THE EL DORADO OF YESTERDAY AND TODAY

California's
El Dorado Yesterday and Today

HERMAN DANIEL JERRETT

PRESS OF JO ANDERSON
SACRAMENTO, 1915

<u>Notice</u>

In many older books, foxing (or discoloration) occurs and, in some instances, print lightens with wear and age. Reprinted books, such as this, often duplicate these flaws, notwithstanding efforts to reduce or eliminate them. The pages of this reprint have been digitally enhanced and, where possible, the flaws eliminated in order to provide clarity of content and a pleasant reading experience.

California's
El Dorado Yesterday and Today

Originally published
Sacramento, California
1915

Reprinted by:

Janaway Publishing, Inc.
732 Kelsey Ct.
Santa Maria, California 93454
(805) 925-1038
www.janawaygenealogy.com

2012

ISBN: 978-1-59641-290-3

DEDICATION

To my dear mother who crossed the
plains with her parents and relatives in
their own train of fifteen wagons, leaving their old home, at Holiday's Cove,
Hancock County, West Virginia, in
March, 1852, and arriving at Cave
Valley, El Dorado County, by the way
of Hangtown and Coloma, September,
1852, this work is lovingly dedicated.

CONTENTS

CONTENTS—Continued.

ILLUSTRATIONS

ILLUSTRATIONS—Continued.

PREFACE.

This work has been prepared with the following design, viz: to rescue from the debris those most important events in El Dorado county history, which not only every Californian, but every American youth should know, and to render a just tribute of renown to the many great and wonderful happenings of the old historic county. Which, coming to an issue at different times, have been decided by the progress of events; and incidentally, to inspire by the sweep of the story, a love for the old county, and an intelligent solicitude for her destiny.

I have treated of times long past, over which the twilight of uncertainty had already thrown its shadows, and the night of forgetfulness was about to descend forever. Year after year I have watched the early history of this old and venerable county gradually slipping from our grasp, trembling on the lips of narrative old age and day by day dropping piecemeal into the tomb. In a little while, the old pioneers, who serve as the tottering monuments of early days, will be gathered to their fathers; their children, of which I am one, engrossed by the empty pleasures or insignificant transactions and happenings of the present age, will neglect to treasure up the recollections of the past, and posterity shall search in vain for memorials of the days of gold and forty-nine.

Determined, therefore, to avert if possible the threatened misfortune, I industriously set myself to work, to gather together all the fragments of the momentous events of the early history of California's El Dorado of yesterday. And it is not without fear of censure that I submit this work to the Sons and Daughters of the pioneers, the Californian, and the American Youth, in the confident belief that, as they study the wonderful history of this venerable old county, they will learn to prize it more highly, and treasure it more carefully, and if the book shall be worthy of a place in a home of the reader, I shall not regret the labor I have given it, nor greatly suffer from the censure its faults may bring upon me.

I am no historian. Neither am I a journalist, but merely a native El Doradoan, who writes in the ardent hope of drawing the attention of the public of America and tourist of foreign climes to a land of which so little is known, respecting its historical importance, fertility, scenic wonders, genial climate, and natural wealth.

In producing this volume, I have consulted the various histories of California and the works of former writers to which I desire to acknowledge my indebtedness.

Thanks are due, also, to the many friends and old pioneers who furnished photographs and such information, thus enabling me to present the chief events whereof I write.   H. D. J.

El Dorado County.

CHAPTER I.

Introduction.

EL DORADO, (el-do-ra-do) the name of the county famous in history as the seat of the first discovery of gold in California by the American people, and the subject of this history, was derived

SUTTER'S MILL AND COLOMA (1851).

from the Spanish eldorado, the Gilded man, the name of a chief of an Indian tribe in South America in the sixteenth century, but since that period has been the subject of all those stories relating to a land of newly discovered treasures.

El Dorado county is situated in the central eastern part of California, and is one of the twenty-seven counties into which the state was divided at its organization, their boundaries being a matter of an act signed February 18th, 1850, with Coloma as the first seat of government of this county. It is bounded on the north by Placer county; on the east by Lake Tahoe, and the state of Nevada; on the west by Sacramento county, and on the south by Alpine and Amador counties. Its total length is 85 miles, its width 35 miles, and it embraces an area of 1,872 square miles or 1,208,080 acres. It is larger than the state of Rhode Island and nearly as large as the state of Delaware.

Having thus briefly introduced my readers to El Dorado county, and given them some idea of its form and situation, they will naturally be curious to know from whence it came, how it was created, and what it contains within its boundaries, and indeed the clearing up of these points is absolutely essential to this history in as much as if California had not been discovered at the time and in the manner in which it was, it is more than probable that the renowned El Dorado, would never have had an existence under American rule. To proceed successfully then it will be necessary to plunge for a chapter or two into the depths of the early history of this State, particularly the part that leads up to the discovery of gold at Coloma, on the American river in El Dorado county.

CHAPTER II.

Early History.

Colonization and civilization must have advanced with peculiar irregularity during the sixteenth century. For we learn from early history that, while the seeds of our social and national existence were being sown in the east and other far-away countries, vast regions of America most inviting and possessing great natural attractions, were entirely neglected or unknown. California, in the far west with its rich soil, genial climate, and balmy atmosphere lay wrapped in primitive solitude, and the first authentic account that we possess of this vast region is derived from the records and writings of early Spanish navigators, who, after Columbus had brought the new world into the family of nations, sought further knowledge of that land, the greater portion of which was still unknown.

In 1501, or nine years after Columbus landed on the eastern shores of North America, Alvarez de Cabral, made known his discovery of Brazil, but the waters of the ocean that washed the golden beaches along the sunset shores of this newly discovered land, had not as yet been seen by European eye; this was reserved for the Spanish adventurer, Balboa, who, in 1513, after making a journey into the interior of Darien (Colombia, S. A.), and from a high mountain peak to which he ascended, he first beheld the peaceful waters of the Pacific. Simultaneously with the entry of Cortez into Mexico in 1519, the Portuguese navigator, Magellan, then in the employ of the Spanish government, effected an entrance into the Pacific ocean through the straits now bearing his name. To this gallant navigator, who was slain at the Philippines in 1520, are we indebted for the appropriate name of this great ocean (Mare Pacificum). One after another the daring navigators and explorers came, and after having explored and settled the greater part of South and Central America, turned their attention to the exploration of the coast of what is now Lower and Upper California.

Cortez, having completed his conquest of Mexico, in 1521, pushed westward to the Gulf of California in 1534, and from that period up to 1540, the date of his final departure for Spain, had made several expeditions in the vicinity of Lower California.

The year 1542, June 27th, fifty years after the discovery of America, found Juan Rodriguis Cabrillo, a Portuguese by birth, in command of two small vessels, the San Salvador, and Victoria, exploring the coast of Upper California. After touching at several points along the coast he was taken ill, died and was buried on the island of St. Miguel off the coast of southern California.

Bartolome Ferrelo, the officer next in command to Cabrillo, believing that it was his duty to carry out the orders given his chief, continued on as far north as Cape Mendocino, named by him "Cape Mendoza" after the Viceroy of Mexico, under whose orders Cabrillo had sailed. He returned in the following April to Natividad, the place of their departure, without having gained much knowledge of the coast, but Cabrillo undoubtedly was the first white man to set foot on California's golden soil.

In 1579, we find Sir Francis Drake, the English navigator, sailing northward along the coast as far as Oregon, but not being able to face the northern gales he was driven back and sought shelter in an inlet near Point Reyes, a short distance north of the Golden Gate, now called Drakes bay, where, not aware that Cabrillo more than thirty years before had discovered and explored the coast of California, he took possession of the country in the name of the Queen of England, Elizabeth.

On May 5th, 1602, another expedition sailed from Acapulco under command of Sebastian Viscaino, who took a northward course and more thoroughly explored the harbors of San Diego and Monterey, which Cabrillo had visited many years before, and exchanged friendly greetings with the natives of this new land.

CHAPTER III.

Settlement of Upper California.

Nearly all of the voyages and expeditions of the sixteenth century were fitted out by zealous Spanish adventurers, for the purpose of discovering the fabled treasures of California, which seemed not to be confined to silver and gold, but also to diamonds and other precious stones. Each expedition, however, failed either to discover the golden treasures of her mountains, or bring to light the splendid harbor of San Francisco, the seal of which was yet unbroken, and, although her mighty Golden Gate had stood ajar since creatures dawn, her charms were still virgin and unseen save by the wild birds, whose fleet course carried them uninterrupted through that portal destined to become one of the world's greatest commercial marts.

The vast region of California, its salubrious climate, rich soil, towering mountains, and mineral wealth, were all unknown to civilized man. No furrow had yet been turned in her broad, rich valleys; no hand had touched her golden treasures; no keel had ruffled her inland waters. All along, from the first discovery of the coast, California was supposed to be an island, and on the maps and charts was called "Islas Carolinas"; and that supposition prevailed until after Father Kino's expedition from Lower California to the waters of the Colorado and across the Gulf of California, in 1702, when it was determined by him that California was not an island, but a part of the mainland of the American continent, and that the Gulf of California ended at the mouth of the Colorado, leaving the land lying west of it a peninsula. Lower California was by this time well settled, and sixteen small missions had been established, under the control of the Franciscan Monks, with Father Junipero Serra as president.

It was on the 1st day of April, 1768, that Serra entered Loreto, the capital of the Missions on the peninsula, and took final possession, by order of King Charles of Spain, who had become jealous of the political influence of the Jesuit Order throughout his dominions, and had the year before, 1767, issued a decree expelling the whole Order from his domain. Under the leadership of the energetic Father, new life was infused into the missionary establishments on the peninsula, and in 1769, we find him with Don Gaspar de Portola, Governor of Lower California, founding new Missions and introducing civilization into Upper California. He established his first settlement at San Diego, July 1st, 1769, and on the 14th day of July, Portola, with a new expedition, started northward from San Diego to locate the Bay of Monterey, which had been discovered by Cabrillo and later explored by Sebastian Viscaino. After a long and tiresome journey, the party reached Monterey where they halted and erected a cross, but, not satisfied that it was the place of which they were in search, they proceeded northward; and on the 25th day of October, 1769, came in sight of the sand hills of the peninsula of San Francisco, with its beautiful bay stretching north and south a hundred miles, landlocked upon all sides save at the narrow entrance of the Golden Gate, connecting it with the Pacific Ocean, and forming one of the finest harbors in the world.

The honor of the discovery of this magnificent harbor, must then be awarded to Gaspar de Portola, and not to Sir Francis Drake, he, as we know from the best authority never saw it; neither can it be assigned to Father Serra, who, with other missionaries, remained at San Diego during Portola's journey northward. This harbor was named by Portola, after the founder of his monastic order,

(Saint Francis), and the first ship to enter through the Golden Gate, was the San Carlos, one of Serra's ships which came from San Diego and explored the bay in all directions in June, 1775, at which time Serra first beheld the Bay of San Francisco. On his return to San Diego, Father Serra directed that a mission be established at this place, and his orders were carried out by Friars Francisco Palon and Bonito Cambon, October 9th, 1776, the date the Mission called San Francisco de los Delores was founded. Serra visited the Mission but once after this and that was from October 1st to 10th, 1777.

CHAPTER IV.

Advancement of California.

A long calm seemed now to hang over California, during which time the Franciscan Friars were in complete control. From 1776 to 1822, a period of nearly fifty years, California was under Spanish sovereignty, and from 1822 to 1846, a period of twenty-four years under Mexican rule. About this time hostilities between United States and Mexico, were threatening over disputed territory which lay between the Rio Grande and Nueces rivers. War was declared against Mexico May 12th, 1846. A United States fleet had already been dispatched to the coast of California under command of Commodore Sloat of the flagship Savannah, who had been advised by the navy department, that war with Mexico might occur, in which case he was, without further notice, to employ his fleet for hostile purposes, and to capture

Monterey, the Mexican seat of government. As other countries had designs on California, Sloat felt he should be watchful lest he should be forestalled. The Savannah and her escorts, the "Preble" and "Cyanne", were at Mazatlan on the Mexican coast, and near by was the English battleship "Collingwood" under command of Admiral Seymour, whom Sloat closely watched. One day

COMMODORE SLOAT LANDING AT MONTEREY, JULY 7, 1846.

Sloat's attention was called to a courier who was bound for the English vessel with presumably important dispatches from the City of Mexico. For upon receipt of this secret information, the Collingwood was made ready for a speedy departure. This led Sloat to believe that war existed between the two countries and he immediately raised anchor and sailed out of the harbor behind the British ship. They were not long outside the harbor when they parted company, the American vessel taking a northward course, and on the 7th day of July, 1846, Commodore Sloat entered the Bay of Monterey, and to his unspeakable delight and relief, found the Mexican flag still floating over the Custom House. Sloat immediately rested anchor, manned the small boats, pulled ashore, demanded the surrender of the place, and hoisted the Stars and Stripes.

Three days later the Collingwood sailed into the bay, there finding at anchor the Savannah and her escorts, and the American flag floating over the Mexican territorial capitol of California. California had now entered upon a new era of advancement. On the 9th day of July, San Francisco, north of Monterey, was taken by a part of the American squadron, acting under the orders of Com. Montgomery, of the Portsmouth. Commodore Stockton arrived in a small frigate, the Congress, on the 15th, and on the 17th Commodore Sloat dispatched a party to the Mission of San Juan, to recover cannon and other munitions of war. The American flag had already been planted at this place a few hours before by Col. John C. Fremont, the conqueror of California, who had the year before been sent out by the government with the ostensible object of making peaceful explorations. Fremont had made two trips to California, and from a study of his diary with the geographical position given, indicated with a certainty that on his first trip he crossed over the Sierras from the Carson valley at a point south, but in view of Lake Tahoe and down one of the branches of the American river through El Dorado county to Sutter's Fort, where he arrived March 6th, 1844, and on the 24th of March headed homeward by the southern route, returning to California again December 10th, 1845.

Being threatened by the Spanish Commandant, De Castro, Fremont aroused all the American settlers located near Sonoma and along the Sacramento river, and with his exploring party of sixty-three men who had accompanied him to California on his second expedition, and the added contingent of local American settlers, he put an end to Mexican domination from around the Bay of San Francisco and northward. This was called the "Bear Flag Revolution" from the flag adopted, it being made of a piece of common sheeting, on which was painted with a sort of black paint, a rude image of a grizzly bear. The grizzly bear was chosen as an emblem, as the mountains of California at this time were infested with large numbers of this species. If let alone the grizzly would attend strictly to his own business, but he would not stand to be made to do that which he did not care to do, nor to have his peace disturbed, and would fight for these rights, and when forced to it he fought his way out or died in his tracks. So it was with the American settlers, who had come to stay; they were quiet and peaceable if let alone. But the Mexicans felt that they could not tolerate the Americans on Mexican territory, and continued to harass them, which resulted in the Bear Flag war.

On July 5th, 1846, the American Californians had declared their independence and placed Fremont at their head, and the Bear Flag floated over all their possessions. A few days later, news reached the California headquarters that war existed between the United States and Mexico, and immediately the Bear Flag was joyfully lowered and the Stars and Stripes hoisted.

Stockton and Fremont continued south with the combined land and naval forces, following General Castro to Los Angeles, a Mexican seat of government, where, the Mexicans withdrawing, they took possession August 13th, 1846, afterwards abandoned and again captured by Commodore Stockton, January 9th, 1847.

General Kearney had by this time made his appearance in California, by way of the southern route, and the conquest of California was at last complete, but by no means in a unified and harmonious state of government. A condition that existed until after the territorial convention was ended and the Constitution signed, November 13th, 1849, at which time Military Governor Riley surrendered the government of the State to Peter H. Burnett, the newly elected Territorial Governor, who held the office until January 6th, 1851, at which time he resigned. This was four months after California was admitted as a State, September 9th, 1850. California can hardly be mentioned as a Territory for it was admitted to statehood before it had territorial representation and recognized as such.

CHAPTER V.

Sutter, His Managers, and Mill.

During all this time California had made but little progress, either in material, social, or moral development; and at the time when it fell into the possession of the United States, by the signing of the treaty of Guadalupe Hidalgo, February 2nd, 1848, with the exception of a few missions and trading posts, was almost as unknown and undeveloped as it was when Cortez first attempted its explorations in the sixteenth century. The entire population of old California in 1840 was estimated at 22,000, of which 5,000 were white people. Los Angeles and Monterey were the Mexican seats of government, and the former in 1846 contained 1,500 inhabitants. In 1850 the census estimate of the population of California was 200,000, an increase of 178,000 in ten years, but the bulk of this increase was recorded during the years of 1848-9-50.

Of all those prominent in the early history of California, but three men concern the reader of this history. They are John A. Sutter, Samuel Kyburz and James Wilson Marshall.

Sutter was born of Swiss parentage at Baden, February 28th, 1803. He was a man of great adventure and many sterling qualities. Leaving his native land he sailed for New York, reaching that

JOHN A. SUTTER.

port in July, 1834. Shortly afterwards he moved
to Missouri and later left for New Mexico where
he learned of California. Here he entered the
employ of the American Fur Company, and win-
tered at their rendezvous in the Kansas Mountains.
Being anxious to explore further into the wild
west, he with several of his comrades started for
California. His route was a long and circuitous
one, for after crossing the plains to Oregon he
found that it would be impossible for him to reach
California as soon as he expected, so he sailed for
the Sandwich Islands, in hopes of getting to California from there, but again failed. Later he embarked to the Island of Sitka, in Russian America,
and from there sailed for the California coast,
reaching Yerba Buena (San Francisco) on the
2nd day of July, 1839. Not being permitted to
land here, he again embarked this time to Monterey, where he was finally allowed to set foot on
California soil. Here he obtained permission of
Governor Alvarado to locate himself in the valley
of the Sacramento. He explored this river and a
short distance up each one of its main tributaries,
the Feather and American rivers, establishing himself on the latter, some distance above its mouth.
Shortly afterwards locating near the confluence
of the Sacramento and American, where in 1840,
he established a little settlement and fort then
known as "New Helvetia", and later as "Sutter's
Fort", situated where Sacramento, the capital of
the State of California, is now located and where
still stands the old historic fort. In June, 1841,
Sutter visited Monterey, and was declared a Mex-

ican citizen, and at the same time was granted
eleven leagues of land surrounding his settlement.

Shortly after the discovery of gold, and the
immense flood of immigrants began to pour in,
his land was forcibly entered upon, under the plea
that they were the unappropriated lands of the
United States, and by 1852, Sutter was broken in
purse, disheartened, and robbed of all his holdings.
Being disheartened he removed to his holdings on
the Feather river, in Sutter county, where he resided until the great flood of 1862, which again
took from him his only support. He went from
here to Washington, D. C., where he sought to
regain title from this government to the land that
had been stolen from him during the gold rush.
In 1873 he removed to Litiz, Pennsylvania, and
on the 18th day of June, 1880, died in the Mades
Hotel at Washington, D. C. Sutter, though unsuccessful and unrecognized, was the man to whom
California, yes, the whole United States owes so
much, and upon whom has been bestowed so little.

Samuel Kyburz was born in Switzerland, in
1810. He came to America with his parents, arriving at New York in 1833, and later moved to
Wisconsin, where he met and married Miss Re-
becca Barber, formerly of Ohio. In the spring
of 1846, he packed up all his movable belongings
and with his family started across the plains,
headed for Sutter's Fort in California, where he
arrived in the fall of 1846, just ahead of the Donner
party. He immediately entered the employ of
General Sutter as his outside manager, and at the

SAMUEL KYBURZ.

same time took charge of the hotel at the fort, in what was later called "Kyburz Annex". Kyburz' duties often compelled him to ride out over the valley and back into the foothills in search of stock, and at the same time becoming familiar with the country, and it was on one of these rides that brought him into the Little Culloomah valley on the American river, where later he directed Marshall to go in his search of timber and a suitable location for a sawmill. After the discovery of gold Kyburz moved to San Francisco, and purchased a vessel, a business venture that caused him great financial loss. He returned to Sacramento, his old home, where he resided until the fall, after the flood of 1862, at which time he moved to Clarksville and located on a large stock ranch and began the business of dairying and stock raising, living here until his death, January 15th, 1898. He was survived by three sons and an even dozen grandchildren, all at that time residents of El Dorado county.

James Wilson Marshall was born in Hope township, Hunterdon county, New Jersey, in 1812, where he learned the coach and wagon builders' trade under his father. After arriving at the age of twenty-one he became restless to travel, and a short while afterwards turned his back on his birthplace, and journeyed westward. He first stopped at Crawfordsville, Indiana, where after several months' stay he found himself not satisfied, so he moved on to Warsaw, Illinois. His stop here was

JAMES WILSON MARSHALL.

very brief and he again moved westward, this time to Platte Purchase, Missouri, near Fort Leavenworth, where he located a homestead and began a farmer's life. About six years later the cry to California met his ears, and being of a restless nature he decided to go. Gathering up his stock and a few belongings, he joined a neighborhood party, and with a train of a hundred wagons they set out overland, about May 1st, 1844. Shortly after starting the party met with heavy storms which considerably delayed them. After reaching Fort Hall, they separated and Marshall with about forty others who had learned that the better way to enter California was by the way of Oregon, took that route. The trip was unaccompanied by any special excitement, and after wintering in Oregon, the party reached California via Shasta in June, 1845, their first stop being at Cache creek on the Sacramento river, about forty miles from Sutter's Fort. Here the party separated, some going to Yerba Buena, now San Francisco; others scattered out over the valley, and a few went to Sutter's Fort. Marshall was among the latter, and in July, 1845, he engaged to work for Sutter, doing general carpenter work. The spring and summer of 1846 was the Bear Flag war period which has already been spoken of and in which Marshall had been a prominent figure. After returning from the war, Marshall immediately went to his holding on Butte creek, which prior to the war he had purchased from one Samuel J. Hensely, but only to find his stock had been stolen and his personal effects pillaged. Not being a man of delay, and after dis-

covering his loss, he immediately decided to enter
the lumber business. Remembering that Sutter
was in need of lumber, he returned to Sutter's Fort,
where he made arrangements with General Sutter
to furnish him an Indian guide and interpreter,

MARSHALL'S CABIN AT COLOMA AND MONUMENT IN THE
BACKGROUND.

that he might cruise along the streams back into
the foothills in search of timber and a suitable
site for erecting a sawmill, and while on this trip
to investigate the place that Kyburz had visited
some time before, and described to him. Having
made up his little party, Marshall set out across
the valley and soon reached the main fork of the
American river, a short distance east of the fort.

MONUMENT ERECTED AT COLOMA TO THE MEMORY OF
JAMES W. MARSHALL.

He followed up the south bank of this stream until
he arrived at the junction of one of its main tributaries, the South Fork of the American. At this
point the hills began to narrow up, forming a canyon, in some places being almost precipitous yet
picturesque. For several days Marshall continued
up the canyon, examining the country on both sides
of the river for a suitable site for his mill. At last
the canyon began to broaden out into a wide basin,
and the river became flat with a snake-like course
winding its way around the low hills between
which were many small, fertile valleys. After
making a careful examination of the locality, Marshall decided that the water-power was abundant,
and that the surrounding hills and valleys were
covered with a variety of thick timber in appa-
rently inexhaustible quantities. He was also satisfied that the lumber from the mill could be trans-
ported to the valley without difficulty, and that
his future success in the lumber business was certain. Having staked out a suitable mill site, on
the south bank of the river at a point where it
made a slight bend to the north, Marshall returned
to the fort, and made known the success of his
trip to General Sutter, at the same time stating he
was without capital but would like to be a partner
with him and assist in the building and operation
of the mill, and Sutter at once accepted his offer
to join him in the undertaking. This was about
June 1st, 1847. Many delays were caused by first
one thing and then another, and the final part-
nership agreement between the two was not drawn
up until about the 19th of August. This agreement

was to the effect that Sutter was to furnish the
capital and Marshall was to superintend the erec-
tion and operation of the mill, and was drawn
up by Sutter's clerk, John Bidwell, and witnessed
by Samuel Kyburz, Sutter's business manager.
Shortly after the articles of agreement were drawn
up and signed, Marshall accompanied by Peter L.
Weimer and family, six or seven mill hands and
several Indians, all of whom Marshall had em-
ployed to assist him, started for the mill site,
where work on the mill was at once commenced.
The names of the white men who accompanied
Marshall besides Weimer and family, were William
Scott, James Bargee, Alexander Stephens, James
Brown, William Johnson, Charles Bennett and
Henry Bigler, most of whom were Mormons and
later returned to Salt Lake. William Scott com-
mitted suicide in a hotel at Georgetown in 1856.

Sutter's mill was of the old fashioned up-and-
down type, and the power of the rushing water
of the river was utilized by means of a water wheel
set in the mill-race, into which the water was
turned by means of a gateway or fore-bay, where
it would strike against the paddles of the wheel
and after delivering its power, continued on
through the narrow channel, uniting with the
waters of the river again just below the mill.
It was in the construction of this narrow channel
that led to the discovery of gold. During the day-
time the workmen would loosen the rock and earth
along the channel, at the same time throwing out
the large size rocks, and at night raise the gate
at the fore-bay, allowing the water to enter and

carry away the sand and gravel. This work had been going on for some time and every morning Marshall would visit the works, and after the gates had been closed and the water ceased flowing, he would walk down the uncompleted mill-race to see what had been accomplished the night before and the day previous.

CHAPTER VI.
The Discovery of Gold.

We are now approaching the most important event of California history, for on the occasion of which we are about to speak, Marshall had strolled to the lower end of the race where he stood for a moment, looking down along the bottom. At this juncture his eyes were attracted to a glittering substance which lay beneath the water in a crevice of the bedrock. He stooped and picked it up. It was of a yellow color, unlike anything he had ever seen before. It must be a mineral of some kind, he thought, and he tried to recall everything he had ever heard, or read about the various minerals and rocks. Then the thought came to him, "could it be gold" as he remembered reading, gold was yellow in color, heavy and malleable. He tried the latter test and then leisurely sought the company of his workmen and made known to them his find. This was on Wednesday, the 19th day of January, 1848, according to Marshall's own statement. The nugget weighed about six penny-weights (or $5.00). After passing a few joking remarks about his gold mine, he proceeded to the residence of Mrs. Weimer, the wife of his foreman,

Peter L. Weimer, and, showing the nugget to her, he asked her permission to drop it into a kettle of soft soap which she was preparing for washing purposes, where he left it for three days. Upon taking it out of the soap, Marshall noted its brightness, and that the lye had not attacked the body of the metal itself. From this and the malleability test he thought it must be gold. Several days later Marshall carried a small quantity of the yellow metal which he and his workmen had gathered, to General Sutter, who examined it without much belief of its value. Considerable doubt still existed among many as to its being gold, and Sutter seemed to have regarded Marshall as insane when he insisted that it was gold. Nevertheless, gold it was, but the news of the discovery did not reach San Francisco until the following spring of 1848, where several specimens of the mineral were exhibited by Charles Bennett. Here Isaac Humphrey, an old Georgian gold miner, saw it, and at sight pronounced it gold. Yet he could not induce any of his friends to accompany him to the new gold fields. Realizing the importance of this discovery, he started alone, arriving at Sutter's mill March 7th, 1848. Later having confirmed his belief as to the nature of the discovery, and at the same time settling the question among the workmen at the mill, he with the rest of the men—who by this time had discontinued their other pursuits—went to digging for the metal which has made California famous.

The news spread with wonderful rapidity, and the year 1849 is a period ever memorable in the

history of California. In the spring of this year
San Francisco had a population of two thousand,
most of whom were waiting for the rainy season
to be over that they might move to the new gold
fields. The summer found it practically deserted,
but it was not long before the settlement was
again flooded with human beings from all parts
of the globe. The news continued to spread. Over
the Rocky Mountains came the eager gold hunters
in long lines of emigrant trains, working their
tedious march over almost precipitous mountains
of eternal snows and arid plains, following the
dusty line of the meandering ox teams, as they
anxiously cast their wistful eyes toward the prom-
ised land in the direction of the setting sun,
leaving behind them the newly made graves, and
the bleaching bones of their famished and over-
burdened brutes, to tell the sad story of their weary
journey, and to mark the path of the early travelers, as they beat their stubborn animals across the
sandy desert of the Humboldt, then over the rugged
Sierras and down the western slope to old Hangtown and on to Coloma, the excited gold camp.
Some came by way of the Isthmus, while others
followed the course of the historic navigator Magellan around the Horn and through the straits.

On, on they came, spreading over the entire
fields of ravines, gulches, and streams of the foothills, where they hastened to make their camps
and stake their claims. Many of the locations
yielded immense fortunes of pure gold with but
little effort or mechanical appliances. During the
year 1846, $10,000,000 in gold had been extracted

from the mines, more than $40,000,000 in the year
1849; $50,000,000 in 1850; and $50,000,000 in 1851.
From January 19th, 1848, the day of the discovery
of gold in California, to the beginning of 1870, the
gold product of the State was one billion dollars,
the bulk of which came from California's El
Dorado of yesterday.

The noted mining camps and bars of "49" and
"50" were: Coloma, Hangtown, Georgetown, Sal-
mon Falls, Greenwood Valley, Cold and Mud
Springs. The bars along the South Fork of the
American river were: Dutch Bar, Kanaka Bar, Red
Bar, Stony Bar, Ledge Bar, Missouri Bar, Michigan
Bar, and Chili Bar at a later date. The Cosumnes
river contained Big Bar, Michigan Bar, Bucks Bar,
Pittsburg Bar, Wisconsin Bar, and later Rocky
Bar. On the North Fork of the American river
were Condemned Bar, Long Bar, and Dotons Bar,
Beals Bar, Horseshoe Bar, Whisky Bar, where the
first wire bridge in the State was constructed;
Oregon Bar, where the main wagon road from
Sacramento, through Salmon Falls, Pilot Hill and
Cave valley crossed to Yankee Jim's, and other
points in what is now Placer county; Vermont Bar,
Browns Bar, Kennebec Bar, Wildcat Bar, Willow
Bar, Hoosier Bar, Green Mountain Bar, Main Bar,
and Poverty Bar, Buckeye Bar, Spanish Bar, Afri-
can Bar, American Bar, Sardine Bar, Drunkards'
Bar, Ford's Bar, Volcano Bar, Sandy Bar, Grey
Eagle Bar, Yankee Slide, Eureka and Boston Bars,
Pleasant Bar, Horseshoe Bar and Junction Bar.
All the above-named bars contained placer gold,

but the richest being those along the North and Middle Forks which alone contributed more than $15,000,000 to the gold production. In most cases the richest bars were found immediately below the confluence of the main tributaries.

During the first ten years after the discovery of gold in California, the efforts of the miners were chiefly directed to mining in the gulches, ravines, and river beds; and every available spot of this class swarmed with thousands of goldseekers, who penetrated every nook and corner in the foothill regions in search of the yellow metal, and with prospecting pan, shovel, and rocker, long-tom, sluice, wing-daming the rivers, sluicing the flats, and sidehills have discovered and pretty thoroughly worked most of the accessible surface diggings. The masses moved in all directions. Cotton-tent villages sprang up as if in a single night, presenting scenes of excitement, activity, and industry. Honesty was a virture with the "49er", and in nearly all camps "Judge Lynch" ruled. They had no time for courts, regulated juries, or lawyers, and he who ventured to take life, or property was quickly met by the hands of a mob, who just as quickly decided that the culprit was a fit subject for the rope, and he was soon left hanging from a limb of the nearest oak tree.

Mining advanced by stages: the pan gave way to the rocker, the rocker to the long-tom, the long-tom to the sluice-way and finally to the hydraulic and powder, which powerful agents leveled the hills and made mining profitable. Then followed the drift mining where tunnels were run into the hills, in some cases thousands of feet, for the purpose of tapping the hidden channels of the ancient rivers of old El Dorado, some of which are buried many feet under the volcanic capping.

Gold, the irresistible magnet, and the pleasures that gold could buy, soon gathered into California's El Dorado, a mixed population of nearly fifty thousand of the wildest, bravest, most intelligent, yet most reckless beings that were ever before or since collected into one small district of country. Many thousand more came and went, and each of them had more or less to do with the building up of the old mining camps, which are ever green in the memory of the early gold hunters, and historical monuments in California history.

CHAPTER VII.

Historical Towns—Sutter's Mill.

At last we have arrived at the little sawmill camp, made up of tents, log cabins, and roughly built houses, formally called "Sutter's Mill", being the place where gold was first discovered by the American people in the State of California, and the early home of the discoverer. The little settlement was soon turned into a bustling camp and became the metropolis of the gold regions. It supported a large population and did a great business, and for a long time remained the principal town. We find no trace of "Judge Lynch" in this town of world-wide notoriety, neither do we find where the place had been visited by the ravages of a general conflagration at any time during its early life; in that respect, being more fortunate than most of her sister mining camps.

Shortly after the discovery of gold, the name "Sutter's Mill" was changed to that of "Coloma", the Indian name of the valley in which it is located (Culloomah), and it became the motto of the day, the longing for millions, whose starting points had been from most every point of the globe. Coloma soon became over-populated, and the oncoming gold seekers, who were journeying in by the thousands, were forced to spread over the entire field of ravines, gulches, and streams of the foothills.

The first business houses in Coloma were the New York Store, conducted by Captain Shannon and Cady, S. S. Brook's Store and John Little's Emporium on the north side of the river. Captain Shannon was the head of the town and its first Alcalda, being appointed by the Military Governor. John T. Little was the first Postmaster, followed by S. S. Brooks.

Coloma was the first seat of government of El Dorado county, made so by a vote of the people, shortly after the county's organization. It was incorporated by act of Legislature April 21, 1856, the act being repealed April 19, 1909. The first newspaper in the town was the "Miners' Advocate", started by James R. Pile & Co., 1851, and purchased by John Conness, Waldron & McConnell in 1853, who changed the name to the "Empire County Argus". The new owners published it for only a short time when the plant was moved to Diamond

Springs in 1854, and there edited by F. H. Snyder.

The mining at Coloma being confined to the ravines and river beds only, was consequently short lived, and in 1854 we find a retrograde movement in the old camp, while the newer camps in the vicinity were rapidly increasing in population.

The following is a partial list of those who were prominent in the early life of old Coloma, not

COLOMA, ON THE SOUTH FORK OF THE AMERICAN RIVER.
The Arrow Points to the Spot Where Gold Was First Discovered.

heretofore mentioned: Newell, Williams, Thomas H. Hewes, A. Van Guilder, and D. P. Talmadge, lawyers. The latter named was later Assemblyman from this district. Tod Robinson, District Judge, 1851; James Johnson, County Judge, 1852 to 1864;

Ogden Squires, County Judge, 1864; B. F. Myers,
District Judge, 1858 to 1864. William McConnell
& Company, merchants; D. G. Waldron, who was
appointed Postmaster soon after President Pierce's
inauguration, the Coloma office being at this time
the principal postoffice in California; David E.
Buel, second Sheriff in the county; E. & S. B. Wel-
ler, tinsmiths; T. Berkhart, gunsmith; R. V. Clark,
butcher; Dr. Gibbs, Thomas Robertson, Robert
Chalmers, General Thomas Williams, W. M. Dona-
hue, afterwards a resident of Placerville, and Hon.
J. C. Brown. Each old mining camp was inhabited
by notorious characters of the under-world. Of
the many that inhabited Coloma we mention but
one, "Texas Ellen", who was ready and willing at
all times to extend a helping hand to the sick and
needy emigrant. Many a poor fellow she helped
to success, and many a sick one she nursed to
health.

During all this time Sutter's sawmill, of course,
stood out as a marked monument of the place and
chief point of attraction for strangers. It had been
finished and was being operated by Winters, Marshall & Bailey, who ran the mill to its utmost
capacity from 1849 to 1853, when it was closed
down and soon went to pieces. During the period
of its operation the stately pines were cut from the
valley and hillsides to supply the great demand for
lumber, which was at that time needed for buildings in the new camps. The prices for lumber,
per thousand feet board measure, were fabulous,
running as high as $500.00 per thousand feet.

Coloma was, up to the discovery of gold, an isolated camp, and the only means of communication between here and Sutter's Fort was by trail, over which all the supplies for the sawmill were carried by pack animals, and horseback was the only mode of travel. But better ways of communication and methods of travel were now necessary to supply the demand of the scattering thousands, that were daily arriving in the new camps. The first road was built from the fort to Coloma, going by the way of Folsom to Mormon Island, a Mormon settlement of 1849, situated a short distance above the junction of the North and South Forks of the American river, then winding its way to the crest of the ridge and along the plateau, passing near the little town of

PINCH-EM-TIGHT,

Which was the name of a miners' trading post, a general store and a few dwellings being the extent of its buildings. It was supported by about five hundred miners, who worked in the ravines and gulches. The camp derived its name from the manner in which "Ebbert", the storekeeper, received his pay for the small articles purchased by the miner. Not having weights small enough to weigh small quantities of gold, he would loosely pinch as much as he could get in this manner from the buckskin sack in which the miner carried it, and each time the miner would yell out "Pinch em tight", hence the name that has followed the place to this day. From here the road descended to the river again, where it passed through the little town of Marshall, and on to Coloma.

MARSHALL,

As it first was called, was situated in the broadest part of the Coloma valley, one and one-half miles below Coloma, where at this time the bed of the river was covered with gold hunters, working their roughly built rockers in search of the yellow metal. The name "Marshall" was changed to that of "Uniontown", 1850, in honor of California being admitted to the Union as a State. The place and its surrounding country had a floating population of more than two thousand, supporting several merchandise stores, a drug store, bakery, hotel, and its quota of physicians and lawyers. It was the home of the second sawmill in the county, and H. K. Stowe was one of the first settlers. In 1853, A. Lohry opened a general store and later erected the brick building that still stands in the old town, now, as of old, used as a general store, wherein is located the present postoffice; and since 1881, at which time the office was established and called "Lotus", the town has gone by that name. Across the river and a short distance below is what is known as

MICHIGAN FLAT,

Once a mining town of that name, with a population of about five hundred. Charles Smith was the proprietor of the first store here, started in a tent in 1849, and it was at this place that the Stanford brothers laid the foundation of their wealth, Thomas W. being the manager of this store.

The dilapidated frame of the old Magnolia Hotel is still visible near the road on the point a short distance up the hill, from the confluence of Greenwood creek and the river.

The old emigrant road had by this time become definitely located, entering the State from Carson valley over the summit by way of Carson pass, down to and across Hope valley, then up the rugged slope of the western summit, over its crest and around the southern end of Silver lake, and down the long but gradual sloping ridges, between the Cosumnes and South Fork of the American river to Diamond Springs junction, then on to Sutter's Fort by the way of Mud and Shingle Springs, Clarksville, and White Rock, and from Diamond Springs to Coloma. Later roads branched off at different points to all the newly settled mining camps in the foothills. The first and most important branch was the one diverging from the old road at a point on the ridge above Sly Park, and running in a northwesterly direction down the western spur of the divide to Sportsman's Hall. From here it followed down the ridge and along Hangtown creek to old

HANGTOWN.

The second old mining camp of importance, formerly called Dry Diggings and later Ravine City, had its origin in the hanging by a mob of two Frenchman and a Spaniard, who had committed a robbery in this old camp. The three men were arrested, tried, found guilty, and hanged to a limb on the leaning oak tree at the corner of Main and

Coloma streets, near the El Dorado saloon, February, 1849. The old tree was felled by Bruce Herrick shortly before erecting the Union Hotel over the spot. The mob rule is again heard of in 1850, when Richard Crone, a desperado and gambler, better known to the community as "Irish Dick", was hanged to a large oak tree on Coloma street, near where the Presbyterian parsonage later

OLD HANGTOWN (PLACERVILLE) IN THE EARLY 50's.

stood, for stabbing and almost instantly killing a new arrival from the far east while he was being entertained by the gambling scenes and wild west ways in the famous El Dorado saloon at the corner of Quartz alley and Main street, where now stands

CARY HOUSE, PLACERVILLE.

the Cary House. "Dick" was well known throughout the old mining camps, but honored Hangtown
most generally with his presence. After having
committed this crime he was taken into custody
by Sheriff "Bill" Rogers, Alex Hunter and John
Clark, Constables of the town, who fought desper-
ately to retain possession of their prisoner, but
against the determined multitude they were power-
less. He was taken from the place where the officers of the law had stationed him, into the street
and tried by a jury of citizens in the presence of
excited thousands.

The verdict was "Guilty", and as soon as it was
pronounced Dick was hurried along with the crowd
to the plaza, where preparations were made for his
execution. At this point the mob were told that
a sick man was in a house near by, and that the
uproar seriously troubled him. The crowd at once
returned down Main street and up Coloma street
to the oak tree where he was hanged. This was the
last time that "Judge Lynch" exercised his power
in old Hangtown.

Killing continued in this town, as elsewhere
throughout the mining camps, but established law
was now in force, and the perpetrators were saved
from the mighty hands of the mob. Like nearly
all old mining camps, this one has not been exempt
from the ravages of the fire fiend. On the 15th
day of April, 1856, it suffered terribly from fire,
when the whole lower portion of the town was laid
in ruins and reduced to poverty, in the course of
a few hours, many who had before been rich.

Again on the 6th day of July, the same year, the town was almost completely laid in ashes, and lives were lost. Nothing better displays the determination of the "49ers", and the recuperative resources of the place than that Hangtown rose again, Phoenix-like, the brighter from its ashes, and is still rising in extent, population, wealth, importance, and stability, and having for its motto, "Excelsior"!

Written words combined with the strongest imagination could not picture the wild scenes of excitement that were daily exhibited on the streets and in the notorious gambling saloons of this old camp.

Hangtown was changed to the name "Placerville" when it was incorporated as a city in the year 1853. Its first Mayor was Alex Hunter, appointed in 1854, followed by George M. Condee, Mayor, and J. M. Grantham, Clerk, in 1856. The daily mail from Sacramento commenced to arrive about the middle of August, 1854, and Placerville soon became a bustling city of some importance. Although old Hangtown is credited with several incidents of mob rule during her early life; although her streets were scenes of wildest excitement; although her buildings were of the rough and ready type, yet no town in the west is surrounded with early history equal to that of old Hangtown. She can boast of having been inhabited by many men who were then or in later life became prominent, a few of which are herewith mentioned: The Hon. B. F. Keene was prominent in early day politics and one of the town's most

honored citizens; he was elected State Senator in
1851, was twice honored by his colleagues with the
election to the Presidency of the Senate, and just
before his death, September 5, 1856, was nominated
to the office of State Treasurer; Thomas A.
Springer is credited with introducing the first
newspaper in the county as well as this city, the
"El Dorado Republican", 1851, and in 1854 he sold
out to D. Gelwicks and W. A. January, who changed
the name to the "Mountain Democrat"; J. L. Per-
kins, one time County Treasurer, made his home
on Piety hill at the intersection of Sacramento and
Benham streets.   The first store was started in
1848 by Mr. Beaner, and Thomas Nugent was the
first Postmaster in old Hangtown, followed by J.
F. Pinkham.   Alex Hunter built the first brick
store in 1849, at which time Col. A. W. Bee and
brother were the leading merchants.   To Col. J.
B. Crandell is due the honor of operating the first
stage line across the mountains, in the summer
of 1857, running a six-horse Concord coach.   John
Kirk and Walter M. Reynolds constructed the first
water ditch to old Hangtown.   The leading business houses in the early fifties were conducted by
George Roth, James Baily, Burns & McBride, A.
Darlington, B. D. Mason, Hunt & Chase, and Louis,
grocerymen; Henry Rapheal, Mark Levison, Abe
and Rudolph Seligman conducted the leading clothing stores.   The last named later founded the
bank of J. & W. Seligman of New York and Seligman Brothers' bank of London.   Tannueau was
the founder and proprietor of the Round Tent
Clothing Store, followed by P. Silbermann & Com-

OLD OHIO HOUSE, PLACERVILLE.
Sacramento Street Entrance.

pany, and later by M. Simon. H. Louis & Company
ran a gent's furnishing goods store, where A. Mierson secured his first position upon his arrival in
Placerville, and later became a member of the firm
of Mierson & Jewell, dealers in gent's furnishing
goods and founders of the A. Mierson Banking
Company's bank. The first hardware store was
run by H. C. Hooker, followed by Jacob Nackman
and I. H. Nash. Dr. F. Childs and Worthen kept
the first drug store, followed by R. White, and
Charles Pettit was proprietor of the Miners' Drug
Store. A. A. Van Voorhies, later of Sacramento,
was the leading saddler. Of the leading hotels
there were the Empire Hotel and theater, conducted by O'Donnell & Russell; the Orleans Hotel,
later the Ohio House, by D. W. La Van, and later
by F. A. Hornblower; the Union Hotel, northeast
corner of Main and Coloma streets, Bruce Herrick,
proprietor; the Mount Joy House, where later the
Western Hotel stood, C. W. Mount Joy, proprietor;
the Cary House, erected by W. N. Cary and conducted under the firm name of W. N. Cary & J.
W. Cullen; the St. Louis House, Theo Wickman,
proprietor; the Motzer House, conducted by Mr.
Motzer; the New York House, conducted by Charles
Hilbert; the Brian Hotel, H. F. Brian; the Cedar
Ravine Hotel, by Frank Freeman; the Rankin
Exchange on Sacramento street, next to the corner
grocery, conducted first by a man named Rankin
and later by Ed. Alderson; the Esmeralda Hotel, on
the creek just back of the Ivy House, Seth Murphy,
proprietor; Tinniman's Restaurant, located in the

center of the block above the Cary House, being the starting point of the fire of 1856. Henry N. Tracy was an expert bookmaker, who received orders from many of the Congressmen and other prominent men throughout the county, and the founder of the present Tracy Shoe Store. J. W. Hines was the old-time blacksmith with whom J. M. Studebaker, America's foremost manufacturer of vehicles, got his first start in California, making miners' wheelbarrows at $10.00 apiece. Joe Douglass was the gold buyer of the camp. Alfred Bell was the proprietor of the famous Boomerang saloon, and "Jack O'Clubs" Philenthol was a noted pawnbroker. B. D. Bingham, F. F. Barss and A. C. Arvidson were the leading jewelers. Mat Messler, opposite the Mount Joy House, and J. R. Munsing, just above in the same block, and Thomas Castile, on Forty-nine corner, were the leading butchers. John Fountain ran the first soda works. Steven T. Gage operated a pack train across the mountains, transporting freight from Placerville to Carson and the silver camps in Nevada. Mr. Gage was a prominent citizen of old Hangtown, and later Vice-President of the Central Pacific Railroad Company, during the time that Leland Stanford was its President. F. F. Barss, Charles Weatherwax and John and James Blair are names familiar as household words to the residents of Placerville, the first a prominent jeweler, the second named a son of an old pioneer business man of Mud Springs, and the last named were old-time sawmill men in this county, and the early proprietors of the old tavern known as "Sportsmen

Hall", John being the first to open this station,
which during the silver excitement fed and housed
thousands of teams and persons daily en route from
California to the Nevada mines. Swift was man-
ager of the Pioneer Stage Company, and Hank
Monk, "Curley Dan" (B. B. Burch), "Coon Hollow
Charlie" (Charlie Saddle), Charlie Watson, and Ned
Blair were some of the noted pioneer stage drivers.

Of the noted women characters, "Emigrant
Jane" and "Ann Mathews" were many times
praised for their charitable work, the former having been known to give at one time $250.00 to-
wards helping a poor family in Upper Town.

A short distance above the old camp on Hangtown creek, was Upper Town, which in the early
mining days was a lively little camp, at that time
separate but now a part of the old town. Those
prominent in a business way were: Jesse Yarnell,
and Turnbull, the leading grocers; I. H. Nash ran a
hardware store, and Howett & Burnham, T. Wil-
cox, S. N. Woods & Co., C. N. Hartwell, and Sill
& Mecham were general merchants; C. W. Brew-
ster & Co., bankers and merchants; Ben Mecham
had a dry goods store; L. J. & McBurton were the
proprietors of the Nevada House, and Edw. Ross-
man, of the Washington House, and George Stout,
and Ben. Putoff were also hotelkeepers here.
Nick Wonderly was the proprietor of a hotel first
and later a blacksmith and wagonmaker's shop.
A man by the name of Garrett had a drug store,
and F. W. Kuhn was the physician and surgeon of
the place. Woods ran a livery stable, and Jacob

Zeisz was the proprietor of the California Brewery, and there was an early day restaurant called the "Mule Restaurant".

In the vicinity of old Hangtown were many small camps, such as Coon Hollow, a camp located on Weber creek just south of Hangtown. Smith & Morrell conducted a grocery store here. Dr. McClenic had a drug store, and the Champion Hotel was the popular house. Little can be learned of the early life of this old camp. There were also Ring Gold, New Town, Iowaville, Dog Town and Fairplay situated on the road from old Hangtown to the southern part of the county.

Hangtown creek passes directly through the town, and was the scene of exciting mining times and a guide for the pioneer gold hunters who crossed the plains and the snow-capped Sierras, by the emigrant route, which was practically the same route that Fremont followed on his first visit to this coast. Old Hangtown was the first town on the road after entering the State, and therefore the entrepot for all the weary immigrants bound for the new gold fields. The first overland mail stage entered the town from the far east Monday, July 19th, 1858, with a most hearty welcome by its residents. After three years' struggle for the county seat, in which Coloma, Placerville, Georgetown, Diamond Springs, and Greenwood Valley were aspirants for the place, Placerville finally came out victorious, by an act of Legislature February, 1857. The population of old Hangtown rose and fell with the immigration, at times having a population of five thousand, then

becoming practically depopulated. In the spring
of 1850 the inhabitants of this place scarcely dared
to hope that their village would ever attain a greater dignity than that of a temporary mining camp,
and even yet, with its picturesque location, historical importance, and pleasant surroundings, not all
the citizens of this old town fully appreciate the advantages of the place. It is true, the town has an
old and "settled" appearance, even to this day, with
its rows of low, quaint brick buildings and streets.

The following lines were written on a sheet of
paper by William Frank Stewart, April 19th, 1865,
the day of President Lincoln's funeral, and pasted
on a pane of glass in a window of an old log cabin,
erected on the south bank of Hangtown creek in
1848, afterwards purchased from the man who
built it by Benjamin F. Post, 1849. The old cabin
stood below the present foundry, and was torn
down about 1862, with no thought of its historical
importance.

> "Touch me gently, friend of mine;
> I'm all that's left of '49'.
> Many a long forgotten face
> Hath watched me in my good old place;
> Many a heart once true and warm,
> Hath watched through me the threatened storm;
> A moral on my face is cast
> Which all must truly learn at last.
> Man's hopes and fears are all, alas!
> Like me, a fractured pane of glass."

This branch of the old immigrant road connected at Hangtown with the branch from Diamond
Springs junction to Coloma, going by the way of

a trading post known as Middletown, situated on
Hangtown creek about two miles below Hangtown,
then passing through the old town of

COLD SPRINGS,

One of the "49" camps, and half-way station
between Hangtown and Coloma. This camp derived its name from a spring of cold water that
forms the source of Cold Spring creek. Mining
was the chief attraction here as elsewhere, and
by 1852 the population had increased to more than
two thousand souls, and fifteen hundred votes
were cast here at one election. The first store and
hotel were opened by Norton & Montgomery, and
Leland Stanford managed a branch store at this
place in connection with his brother's store at
Michigan Flat. Duncan also kept a store here; so
did Dewett & Taylor, and Sudson & Goodenough;
David Miller ran a hotel, and another was run by
a man named Reed. Other men of prominence
were Dr. D. T. Stevenson, Dr. Buttermore, A. Col-
grove, G. W. Paddock, F. Russell, W. W. Penton,
J. M. Goetschius, who was the first Postmaster
here; A. O. Bowen, John Lamb, G. Griffin, M. Con-
aha, Jesse C. Fruchy, J. M. Lockwood, S. N. Perrin,
I. S. Miller, S. Heath, and J. M. Powers. Besides
the stage line to Coloma and Hangtown, there was
a direct daily stage connection with Sutter's Fort.
But Cold Springs was never a commercial center,
and as soon as the surface mines commenced to
play out, the population began to shrink and finally

the stages left this route, and the old camp sank
into desolation.   The next town of importance on
this road was

GOLD HILL,

Another old camp with a population of more
than a thousand, which supported two hotels, two
grocery stores, express office, telegraph and postoffice, butcher shop and several saloons.   The
name of the first hotel was the Gold Hill House,
first opened by a man named Rankin, in 1854,
afterwards leased by Mrs. R. T. Kimble, who conducted the place until 1857.   The name of the
other hotel was the Steve Hill House, the name of
the proprietor, and the man who planted the first
fruit trees at this place, about the same time that
fruit trees were planted at Coloma.   A man by the
name of Chase opened the first store, and the
bakery was run by George Marquart and partner,
and the butcher shop by J. W. Anable.   James
McCormack was the first express agent at this
place, afterwards agent at Mud Springs, and of
late a member of the firm of Seltzer & McCormack
of Redding, California.   H. B. Newell, a prominent
man here and Assemblyman from this county in
1867, was killed at Georgetown during the big fire
and explosion at that place, June 16th, 1898.

Leaving Gold Hill the emigrant route followed
along down the ridge on the left side of Chuck ravine to Coloma, from which point roads were being
built to Kelsey, Louisville, Spanish Flat, American Flat, Georgetown and surrounding camps.
At the same time a road was constructed direct

from Coloma crossing the bridge erected in 1851 by E. T. Raun, to north Coloma, from which place it ascended to the top of the hill, then descending to Alabama Flat and Johntown creek, following up this creek to

JOHNTOWN,

MINING SCENE IN THE EARLY 50's, NEAR GARDEN VALLEY.
(Left to right—Alex Moherter, — Wing, Fred Isebelle and — Worley. Party in Righthand Corner Unknown. H. W. Russell in Front with Pan, Showing Gold.)

Named after a German known as "Dutch John," but now called Garden Valley, which, in 1852, had become quite a rival to the camps of secondary importance on the Georgetown divide, owing to the large number of miners working the beds of Manhattan, Empire and Johntown creeks, the two former being the main tributaries to the latter named creek. The first mining was done at this place in 1849 at a point on Johntown creek, long known as Stony Point. The creek and ravines of this old camp were very rich, yielding very coarse gold, one piece weighing as much as $1500.

The name "Garden Valley" was given to the place at a Fourth of July celebration and dinner, the tables being supplied with vegetables gathered from the gardens along the little valley, which suggested the name. This name, however, was not adopted until some time later, when the postoffice was established, the camp being called "Upper and Lower Johntown", the Upper town being located at the junction of Manhattan and Empire creeks, and the Lower town a little south and west of the present town. The camp at an early election polled over four hundred votes, and was visited and destroyed by fire in 1857, never again flourishing, for by this time the rich placer mining had practically ceased.

From the junction of Manhattan and Empire creeks down to D. W. Fox's ranch, a distance of over a mile, Johntown creek ran through a beautiful pasture vale, and if it had never been disturbed during the early mining days it would have been most valuable for agricultural pursuits, spreading from foothill to foothill, well watered, soil rich and productive, climate mild, snow seldom covering the ground. The creek bottom was rich in gold and its whole length and breadth has been worked over and over again with paying results. The ground along the creek bottom has since been patented and the owners are refilling and leveling the bottom from the rich soil of the sidehills, and ere long it will resume its former beauty and agricultural richness.

Thomas McConnell and brothers were the proprietors of a large general merchandise store, a hotel and a nearby sawmill. Other storekeepers were Jake Smith and Putnam, and Ciperano Pedrini (better known as Bill Tell), and Massimino Pedrini (predecessor to R. Fillipini & Co.) prominent business and stock men of later date. Beatty, Robinson, and Lawrence Wade were among the early hotelkeepers.

The noted quartz mines in this vicinity were the old Taylor, the Esperanza, and Rosencranz. D. W. Fox, W. H. Russell and N. D. Burlingham were also prominent early day citizens.

From Upper Johntown the road followed up the old ridge between Manhattan and Empire creeks, to old

GEORGETOWN,

Which was named after one George Phipps, who first pitched his tent at the head of what since has been called Empire canyon. It was first settled in August, 1849, in this narrow ravine about one-eighth of a mile from its present location. On July 14th, 1852, the whole of the business portion of the town was swept away by fire. Before the ashes had cooled the spirit of California Americans

arose like a star in the midst of her desolation;
the residents of the town resolved to rebuild, and
nobly was it seconded by the miners from the
neighboring camps to change the site of the old
town and rebuild it on the top of the ridge where
it now stands. The new town soon assumed a

GEORGETOWN IN THE EARLY 50's.

substantial and beautiful appearance, and a most
attractive mining town, justly called the pride of
the mountains, was imbeded in the native wilds
of surrounding material wealth, made up of log
cabins, shake houses and canvas tents. In July,
1856, another disastrous fire occurred which destroyed most of the business houses, and many
dwellings. Again in August, 1858, a fire occurred
which swept off about one-half of the business
places, the most damage being done on the east

side of Main street, which was only partially rebuilt. This town was again visited by the fire fiend on May 26th, 1869, which partially destroyed the west side of the main street, including the Catholic church and town hall. The fire started in the Miners' Hotel, and Mrs. Stahlman, the wife of the proprietor, three children and a Miss Stanton perished in the flames. The town has several times since been destroyed by fire, but each time, as before, the indomitable spirit of the people arose in triumph over their misfortune, and Phoenixlike from its ashes the burnt portion was rebuilt.

Notwithstanding these several conflagrations and the changes which followed, the town at the present writing will compare favorably with any of the mining towns of early days. "Judge Lynch" seems to have visited this old town on several occasions, but only once did he hold his usual oak tree picnic. This was in the fall of 1850, when a man by the name of Devine was hanged to an oak tree for shooting and killing his wife, while in a drunken frenzy, because she would not return to him nuggets he had given her, that he might gamble them away. The oak stood near the trail leading from the old town down the ridge to the mouth of Empire and Fools canyon, and he was buried at the base of the tree. Although the town had been notorious for stage robberies and burglaries, incidents of an exciting character have been quite rare. Mining in this district was first confined to the canyons and gulches, and to the bars on the Middle Fork of the American river. Then came the "Hill Diggings", worked by drifting. Tne first of these noted camps was Bottle Hill, opened up in 1851, Mameluke Hill, in 1852, with an output of over $4,000,000; Cement Hill in 1853, and Jones Hill in 1854. Mt. Gregory, where Stanford brothers, Hub McCoy and others were the leading business men; and Volcanoville was started up at about the same time. At each of these noted mining camps thriving towns were built up, and regular stage and telegraph communication with Georgetown was established. But the days of wild excitement have passed by, and an era of permanency apparently has followed with a more general disposition to settle down and work in earnest and thoroughly what has been left from the period of the first excitement and rapid exhaustion, which soon scattered those engaged in working these old camps, and houses left without proprietors, one after the other disappeared, until now not a vestige of a house remains. The old townsites have long been obliterated and the ground upon which they once stood is now covered with a thick forest of pines and manzanita brush. Like Coloma and Placerville, Georgetown was the metropolis of the whole divide upon which it is situated, and she was not far behind her sister camps in furnishing material for representatives to the halls of the State government and the United States Senate.

Of the important men and those prominent in early business life in this old camp we have to name United States Senator Cornelius Cole, who mined here in 1849-50; John Conness, of the firm

of Conness & Reed, merchants, a resident here
from 1849 to 1864. He was one time Assemblyman, State Senator, and later United States Senator, and unsuccessful candidate for Governor;
J. W. McClury, United States Representative and
later Governor of Missouri, also kept a general
merchandise store here in 1852; J. G. Carpenter
was an attorney-at-law, a member of the Assembly
in 1856, and later moved to Placerville, where he
practiced law and became interested in the "Mountain Democrat", a local paper.

The first house in old Georgetown was a log
cabin, erected by Graham & Hull, about September
20th, 1849, in which the first store in the camp
was opened under the name of Graham & Hull.
Little & Company of Coloma opened a branch store
here shortly after in connection with their Coloma
store. Other merchants at this time were Cushing
& Grammar, Tom Clagg, and J. W. Selette. By
1850 the trade and travel had increased and the
business portion more than doubled in area. Hotel
after hotel was built along the hillside above the
stores. There was the Missouri House, kept by a
man named Chance; the Illinois House, kept by
McKinney, and the Alabama by Real. Further
up toward the present townsite on Main street
was Conness & Reed's store, Van Guilder & Hunter's express office; Humphrey & Cunningham,
Stelle & Headley had general stores, and the Round
Tent Gambling House, northwest corner of Main
and Orleans streets, was kept by Pete Valere and
later by Charles Lusks, where N. Luthin, formerly
leader of the Luthin Band of New York, furnished

entertainment. This place was in close proximity
to the Bee House of the same character, run by
Joe Brown, and directly opposite on Orleans street
was Zeke Morey's gambling resort. After the fire
of 1852, Conness & Reed built in the new town
on the lot later occupied by the White Side Hall.
The new town from the foot of Main street to
Orleans street was gradually built up on both sides.
Four hotels were immediately erected: the Nevada
House, D. C. McKenny, proprietor, later conducted
by Marsh and then by Hub McKoy; Reals, the
Georgetown Hotel, the Union Hotel, I. B. Harding,
proprietor; and the Miners' Hotel, E. Robinette,
proprietor; and a Portuguese hotel. W. Wing
Oliver published a newspaper here called "The
Georgetown News". It was a Whig paper, later
published by Pratt & Shaw. McCallum was formerly connected with this paper. Moses J. Warren
was a prominent house builder and mill man and
proprietor of a sawmill on Travers creek. He
afterwards built the Clipper sawmill above Georgetown in company with H. Sornberger, who later
became a prominent business man of this place,
the business still being conducted by his late wife.
Heismans, P. W. Cunningham & Dowdles, Gibbs,
DeTurk & Williamson were liverymen. In 1853
Williamson sold his interest to Daniel Jerrett, who,
in the early '60's, opened a general merchandise
store on the corner of Main and Orleans streets.
Glassman & Forester, J. Cunningham, R. Balm-
forth and G. Fountain were also liverymen; W.
Benjamin was the leading saddler, S. Bloom, O. H.
Burnham, Jacob Goldstein, H. Kohn, Jackson &

Brothers, William Hart, E. Jacobs, Lovinski Brothers, James McCoy, and Charles Orelli were the leading merchants. John I. Spear, banker. Of the leading druggists there were Dr. T. Turner, Cunningham and S. Alden; J. Blackwell, J. G. Carpenter, and Williams & Eastman, attorneys; C. Fredericks, W. L. Thomas, and Spencer, physicians; Burr & Spencer, dentists; A. Burrnie, tailor; C. Clark, Henry Hailton, Charles Karpstein, William Schooley, J. Stevens, and George Ricci, butchers; H. Gill, John Murry, Nelson Owens, George W. Fairhurst, and W. T. Gibbs, blacksmiths; the first marriage celebrated in Georgetown was that of W. T. Gibbs to Mrs. Cynthia Turner, November 10th, 1851. G. Mangold, Jacob Miller, Steinwitz, and Swartz & Company, bakers; William Snyder, brewer, and Joseph Swift, proprietor of the first soda works. Louis Bryant was a prominent citizen and for many years Supervisor of El Dorado county. S. A. Berry and George Handy were also prominent citizens of this place, the latter being a sawmill man. Mrs. Dr. Day taught the first school in the town, and Miss Minerva Hursford the first public school. E. L. Crawford was for many years minute clerk of the Assembly, and also assistant secretary of the Senate. He was also editor of a small paper published in this town in 1872 called the "Gem".

Those prominent in the near-by camps were; Jim Klipstein and Benjamin Keyser, Pierson & Pratt, storekeepers of Mamaluke Hill fame; Sherman Castle, Thomas B. Patton, Twitchel & Com-

pany, who built a large cabin on the ridge between
Oregon and South canyons, north of the since
famous Bull and Mamaluke Hill diggings; A.
Berry, Ben C. Currier, John Wagnor, William Reid,
Alex Connell, George Beattie, Henry Garsy, Jacob
Enri and a man named Hudson, discoverer of the
famous Georgia Slide mines, were among those
who worked in the gulches and surrounding canyons.

At Georgia Slide there were Thomas Bowman,
storekeeper, predecessor to George H. Barklage;
Alex A. Hyatt, Nelson Owens, and P. N. Spencer.
This mine was divided into three claims, the Blue
Rock, worked by Joe Roe; the Pacific, by John
Harden & Company; the Beattie, owned and
worked by John, George, and David Beattie, John
Thurston and Barney Hughes. George Jinks kept
a store at Bottle Hill, and the men connected with
the Pilot creek ditch, built in 1853-4, were Thomas
Wrenn, D. C. McKinney and John Hardin; and the
old California Water Company, constructed in
1852-3, were Cunningham, Conness, Thomas Reed,
and Dr. W. N. Stone.

Daily stages had now (1850) commenced to
run from Coloma to all these camps, the first plying between Sutter's Fort and Coloma, and later
uniting with Graham's line to Georgetown.

Old Coloma, how rapidly she grew, sending
out her six pony expresses a day, which carried
the mail to the various camps. How glad the
miner welcomed the rider and paid his dollar for
a letter from far away home. Perchance it was
evening, and he had been sitting before his cabin

door, chatting with comrade or stranger, or per-
haps making the woods ring with some old-time
melody.

Think of the wild scenes of early California
life which, for so many years, were enacted in the
vicinity of the discovery of gold.   Many a poor
fellow, after a year's hard labor and deprivation,
found himself without a dollar; clothes, health,
hopes all gone; far from home, dispirited, disap-
pointed and in receipt of a letter from wife or fond
ones at home, making urgent appeals for help,
or anxiously imploring their return, reminding
them of their promise when leaving, that they
would be absent only six months or a year.

It was not until 1854 that Placerville was directly connected with Georgetown, at which time
the Stevens, or Pioneer Stage Company, began
operating a line of stages between the two camps.
The old road on which they traveled followed down
along the crest of the point some distance above
the present grade to the river, and crossed on the
old bridge a short distance above the present
structure.   After crossing the river it took a
down-stream course, and up the first long, open
point below the bridge, then followed along the
top of the ridge to the present road crossing at
Texas ravine and on to the old town of

KELSEY,

One of the mining camps still of the old-fashioned
type, situated about six miles from Placerville,

which, during the early mining days, was a lively
little camp, but like the rest of those not commercially located, upon the failure of its rich placer
diggings, the population decreased very rapidly
from thousands to hundreds, and then to a very
few, and now it is but a mere shadow of its former
self. The first store in the town was kept by

HOUSE ON LEFT, OLD UNION HOTEL, HOME OF JAMES W.
MARSHALL, IN WHICH HE DIED AUGUST 10, 1885.

Samuel Smith in 1849 and '50, and Dr. Paul ran
the first hotel. A. Siesnop was also an old-time
hotelkeeper at this place. Other prominent men
here of later date were Patrick Kelly, William Rob-
erts, — Allen. The Union Hotel was run by Mrs.
Reynolds, and Tom McManus was a noted storekeeper. The town was destroyed by fire in 1853, and
partly destroyed by a big blaze on New Year's day,

1856, the beginning of the same year that Placerville, Georgetown and Diamond Springs fought
against the destructive flames. Kelsey was the
mother camp to many smaller ones in the vicinity,
such as Louisville, Columbia, Irish Creek, American

MARSHALL'S OLD BLACKSMITH SHOP AT KELSEY.
As a Typical Miner's Cabin.

Flat, Chicken Flat, Spanish Flat, Stag Flat, Barley
Flat, Union Flat, Peru and St. Lawrenceville. Of
all these not more than two or three houses remain
in each place.

The prospect of a future keeps life in the old
town, and promises her a steady growth, and it

will always live in history, for it was the home of Marshall during his last days, and the place of his death. His old blacksmith shop still stands here alongside the road at the southern entrance to the town, unnoticed, unappreciated and fast going to pieces. After leaving this old camp the road passed through Louisville, Spanish and American Flats, and along the rich Dry Creek valley to Georgetown.

Shortly after the stage line had been started to Georgetown, the same company inaugurated a new tri-weekly line from Placerville to Amador county, August 1, 1854, going by the way of

DIAMOND SPRINGS.

Although Diamond Springs was one of the earliest stopping places on the old Emigrant road, it did not come into prominence as a town until 1850, at which time a party of Missouri emigrants camped here for several days to pasture their stock, and discovered minerals in paying quantities. This brought a rush to the place, and the town followed, increasing in a short while to a population of several thousand.

Destructive fires visited the town on August 5th, 1856, and again on September 23rd, 1859, thus bringing her third in line with Placerville and Georgetown in fires as well as in the election to change the county seat from Coloma. The town derived its name from several springs of pure, clear, sparkling water in the vicinity of a quartz ledge which cropped out on the hill back of the camp.

The men of business and prominence during her exciting days were N. K. Shearer, Postmaster; C. B. Patterson, George M. Waugh, Samuel Haskett, J. H. Haines, Dr. S. F. Hamm, Matthew Arnold, S. Sims, Dr. S. F. Marquis, H. H. West, F. S. Davenport. Henry Larkin was a prominent citizen of this place, as was C. F. Irwin, attorney-at-law, and in 1867 was elected Judge of the County Court of El Dorado county. Mr. Irwin was one of the few survivors of the steamship Tennessee, which was wrecked at the entrance to San Francisco harbor March 6th, 1853. C. P. Morrill was a druggist, and T. Boyle, W. S. Day, N. Rhine, J. Ullman, Kauffman, William Harris and Thomas Farneringham were the general merchants of the camp. J. R. Fuller ran the meat market, Young & Allen kept a hotel, and Peter Schiff, who conducted a blacksmith shop at this place, was one of the old-time settlers.

Five miles further on is the old town of

MUD SPRINGS.

This old town got its name from the springs near its present location, which were used by the emigrants as a watering place for their stock. This caused the place to always be in a muddy condition, and was known by the early travelers as the "Mud Springs", hence the name of the old town. The mining activity of this camp dates back as early as 1849-50, and owing to its location on the main road to the valley and Sutter's Fort, and the richness of its quartz and surface mining in the neighborhood, it ranked in importance and population with the other early mining towns of the county. The town was incorporated in 1855, at which time the name was changed to El Dorado. Some of its prominent business men were J. M. B. Weatherwax, general storekeeper; Charles Boyd, proprietor Oriental Hotel; Wesket & Atmore, proprietors of the Nevada House, and C. P. Roussin, of the Richmond House; J. J. Dean, C. P. Jackson & Co., J. W. Jackson, M. Lasky, Jacob Leiser, William Price, Nathan Rhine, Thomas Russell, and D. Woolover and Aba Wrehner were also popular merchants; Blanchard and Meridith, and Moses Tebbs were the leading attorneys, and Thomas Fitzgibbon, Edward Martin, S. M. Stillwell were butchers; H. D. Hinman, S. Marotte, musicians; Fleming & Company, and S. F. Rogers & Company, lumber dealers; D. Thornton, saddler, and John Theisen and Joseph Luttwig, brewers; Smith & Company, liverymen, and there was an array of bakeries, blacksmith shops and saloons.

From here the road branches, the one to the right being the old emigrant road to the valley by the way of Shingle Springs, another old camp that has stood the test of years, and the road to the left taking a southerly course through the county to Logtown and the forks of the Cosumnes and to Yoemet, the most southerly mining camp in the county, settled in 1851.

Returning to Placerville we find that in 1856 George C. Hanclin & Company were operating a stage line between here and

INDIAN DIGGINGS,

A town of no little consequence in the early '50's, and the home of many Indians who were mining here for some time before the whites made their appearance in 1850, at which time the native miners were discovered, hence the name of the place that soon grew to prominence in the county. The town is about twenty-five miles southeast of Placerville, near the southern boundary of the county. Indian creek passes within the town limits and was unusually rich. By 1856 the camp had reached the height of its prosperity, with a population of more than fifteen hundred, that supported nearly a dozen stores, several hotels, and saloons, drug store, fraternal orders, in fact, a camp with every convenience that a thriving town could afford in the early days. Some idea of the travel into this old camp may be formed by the number of stages running between the town and Sacramento, there being two daily and one tri-weekly, besides the one to Placerville. Indian Diggings was a place noted for something more than its gold, it being the home of the marble beds used for building and ornamental purposes, which are waiting for capital to further develop. The town was several times visited by fire and totally destroyed August 27th, 1857, and partically destroyed in the year 1860. One of the first hotels was run by J. W. Gilmore, who was also Postmaster. Others who lived here during the town's prosperous times were Hall & McPherson, hotelkeepers; W. & S. Grubbs, T. D. Heisquell, P. Gib-

son, G. & J. McDonald, H. C. Sloss, L. S. Bell,
J. R. Head, B. R. Sweetmond, J. G. Busch, A. Riker,
J. S. Lock, J. P. Cantin, R. H. Reed, John Cable,
John Patterson and A. J. Lowry, later of Placerville. Indian Diggings was not behind her sister
camps politically, for she sent to the Legislature,
as representatives of El Dorado county, the following: George McDonald, Tyler D. Heiskell, H. C.
Sloss, John C. Bell, John Fraser, A. F. Taylor and
Thomas Fraser, later Registrar of the United States
Land Office in this State. The old town has followed many of the others, and now—well, she has
assisted the writer in bringing to a close her historical career.

There is yet to mention one other important
branch of the old emigrant route, and that is the
one from Leak Springs Station down the ridge to

GRIZZLY FLATS,

A mining camp of 1851, situated on the high,
heavily timbered ridge between the two forks of
the Cosumnes river, in the southeastern part of
the county. It derived its name from the killing
of a large grizzly bear near the place where the
town was afterwards built, by one Buck Ramsey,
who, with a prospecting party, was searching for
gold in the surrounding hills in the fall of 1850.
In the spring of 1851 good prospects were discovered, and soon the miners began to flock in, and
the camp was not long in becoming a town of some

note. The first fire was in 1866, which partially
destroyed the place, and again a more destructive
fire in 1869. Rich quartz veins as well as the
creek placers were discovered, and they are to
this day the sole support of the town that is far
from its former self. William Knox was one of
the first settlers, and Chris Nelson started the first
store in 1852, followed by A. J. Graham, Hulburd,
and Dean. It had the usual number of saloons, a
butcher shop and a blacksmith shop and foundry.
Of the men sent to the Legislature from El Dorado
county, Grizzly Flats had but one in the person of
James H. Watson, Assemblyman.

We return now to chronicle in its proper order
the road that branched off of the first old road
in the county, that between Sutter's mill and the
fort. This road had the heaviest travel of any in
the gold region. Leaving Sutter's Fort, then called
Sacramento, it followed the old above-mentioned
road to the New York Ravine House, then taking
a northerly course descending to the river, and
crossing at

SALMON FALLS,

Which is located at the mouth of Sweet Water
creek, on the south bank of the American river
about ten miles below Coloma. The town derived
its name from a small fall or cataract in the river,
at which point during the early days, the salmon
could be seen in great numbers. Gold was discovered at this place early in 1849 by a party of
Mormons, who settled here in the fall of '48. R.
K. Berry, who arrived at these diggings in '49 in

company with a few others, set to work in the
spring of 1850 to lay out a townsite, the same being surveyed and platted by P. N. Madegan. It
was at this place that the main road from Sacramento crossed the river, passing through Centerville, Pilot Hill, and Cave Valley to Murderers' Bar,
where it crossed the Middle Fork of the American
river to all the mining camps beyond there, in
what is now Placer county. After leaving Centerville the road branched off and followed up the
divide to Greenwood, Georgetown, and all the
mining camps on this divide. There was heavy
travel over this road during the early period, and
the town of Salmon Falls grew in a short time from
a few Mormon huts to a town of some size, with
a population of about three thousand. The first
residents and business men of the camp were:
R. K. Berry, the first Alcalda, Postmaster, general
merchant and hotelkeeper; — Campbell was a
merchant here, and Thomas Orr, now of Shingle
Springs, conducted a hotel; Abe Richards and E.
T. Raun were residents, the latter being a bridge
builder, and constructed and owned the first
bridges in the county.

But no more is it a town, as it has gone the
way of many of the old mining camps. From
Salmon Falls the road passed Mountain Cottage
and on up the long river grade to

CENTERVILLE (or PILOT HILL),

A relic of pioneer days, which derived its name
from the high nob overlooking the Sacramento

valley, named by Col. Fremont as he passed down
the Georgetown divide on his first visit to California. The old town was first settled in 1849,
and has left to mark its location the old original
hotel, and a short distance north the magnificent
three story brick building built for a hotel in 1860
by A. J. Bailey, at a cost of $30,000, thinking at the
time that it would be on the route of the Central
Pacific railroad, a preliminary survey of which had
just been finished across the mountains this way.
Pilot Hill and its surrounding country is one of
the most beautiful spots in the county, the land
being very fertile and adapted to all classes of
agriculture and stock raising. The celebrated Al-
abaster Cave, discovered in 1860, and the only one
of note in the State, is situated about three miles
below this old town on the road to Rattlesnake
Bar and Placer county. The first house in the
camp was built by Samuel Stevens; Talcott & Rose
opened the first regular store, and John Brown
& Wilson kept the first boarding house; Robert
E. Draper was the pioneer mail carrier, who walked
from Pilot Hill to Sacramento and returned the
same day, carrying mail each way between the
two camps, his rates being one dollar for each letter
and fifty cents for a paper. Other prominent men
of this camp were A. J. Bailey, F. B. Peacock,
David and Thomas Furguson, C. S. Rogers, P. O.
Brown, Thomas Stevenson, formerly of Hoggs
Diggings—a near-by camp of secondary importance
—who is now the largest land owner in this section, including the large brick building above men-

tioned. William Buchan, a former Postmaster and proprietor of the hotel and general merchandise store, and Creque was a hotelkeeper in the building now conducted by S. D. Diel. Leaving Pilot Hill the road followed along a rich and fertile valley to the top of the divide, where it forked, one going up the divide and the other descending to the Middle Fork of the American river. The first place after leaving the junction was the Farnsworth House at Cave Valley, then on to

MURDERERS' BAR.

One of the most noted river bars of the early days, its population being more than five hundred, or large enough to induce Lee & Marshall's National Circus to show here for two days. The bar derived its name—so the story goes—from the murdering by the Indians of a party of early gold hunters. The second wire bridge in the county spanned the river at this camp, later moved to the junction of the North and Middle Forks of the American river. The gold taken from the bed of the river at this place and adjoining bars weighed into the hundreds of pounds, and this is not all, for this old river contains hundreds of pounds more now being sought after. C. Cooledge kept the store and hotel here up to 1855, and E. C. Cromwell, Jim Stewart, George Melville, Col. Potter, William Harrison, Judge Hammond, Phil Herbert, Kemp Anderson, Burton Brothers, Walker Brothers, Col. Kipp, H. C. Glenn, later a resident of Colusa county, were among the first settlers, and "Oregon" Smith owned the toll bridge at the place.

Returning to the forks of the road on top of the hill and following up the divide to Georgetown, the road passed an occasional ranch house, and the Penobscot way station run by L. B. Myers from 1851 to 1854, who later sold to Page & Lovejoy when they purchased from Dr. Thomas the stage line plying between Georgetown and Sacramento, via. Salmon Falls. Many a tired freighter stopped here for the night, and wayfarers lunched on their way to the mining camps beyond

GREENWOOD.

Another old mining camp, located in a little valley originally called "Long valley", through which runs Greenwood creek. The name of the first settlement in this pretty little valley was that of "Long Valley" and later called "Greenwood", after John Greenwood, who opened a trading post here in the spring of 1849. It also was a town of some importance in the early days of gold mining. The first general store was conducted under the firm name of Myers, Fairbanks & Lane. On the 25th of March, 1850, a son was born to Lewis B. Myers, and it is claimed that he was the first child born in the county, but on the same day and year in old Hangtown a son was born to Orlando Shepherd, who on March 31st, 1851, moved to Greenwood, where he spent the balance of his life. A man by the name of Rosteen opened the Buckeye House, the first hotel in the town, and Bloom & Partner kept the Illinois Exchange, afterwards the Nation. Bloom was the first Postmaster of the

place, and John Allen, Harrison, Hilton & Cohea,
John and Robert Sharp, Leeds & Bartlett, H. Lower, George and Jacob Dunn conducted the mercan-
tile houses of the town. William Harris, Stephen
Tyler, C. Foster and John Gleason erected the
first sawmill near Greenwood.

"Judge Lynch" and his followers seemed to have
twice visited this camp, first in 1851, when James
Graham was hanged to an oak tree that stood
in a lot owned by Felice Ricci, for killing a man
by the name of Lesly, and again on July 23rd, 1854,
when Samuel Allen was hanged to the same tree for
the killing of William Shay. The old camp was
far more fortunate than most of the other camps
of the county in the way of destructive fires, there
being but one of any consequence, and that was
in 1856.

Greenwood was an aspirant for the county seat
in the election of 1854, and at one time her population numbered more than a thousand, but since,
like the rest, from the loss of the surface gold and
not being commercially located, she is fast fading
away into the past, and unless some of her rich
quartz veins are developed, she will soon be no
more. So may this be said of her neighbor,

SPANISH DRY DIGGINGS,

Situated on the summit of the ridge about four
miles north of Greenwood, and five miles northwest
of Georgetown, and surrounded by Dutch Bar,
Oregon Bar, Rocky Chucky, mouth of Canyon

creek, all on the river, and the Hoboken House and the Cedarberg Mine on the ridge. The town got its name from the dryness of the ridge on which it stands. Since then water ditches have been constructed to the camp, furnishing its inhabitants with sufficient water for agricultural and mining purposes. This little camp has produced over a million dollars in gold, and the first store in town was opened by Folger, later of San Francisco; Messrs. W. R. Davis, John Hines, T. M. Buckner, " '49ers"; G. W. Hunter, G. W. Simpers, A. Brooke, James K. Esterbrook, Truworth Durgan and Isaac G. Swifth of Georgetown were all prominent in the early mining days of this place.

There were many other old mining camps of secondary importance on the Georgetown and Placerville divides, but since the departure of surface mining many are striving hard to conquer that fate which promises to inaugurate a retrograde movement in their actions, and those that have left our midst entirely are like unto Sutter's mill, no man knoweth the exact spot upon which they stood. Many opportunities still surround these old places, only waiting the tilling of their rich soil and the development of their gold-bearing veins, and it is only hoped that the deplorable condition of these old camps will be overcome in the near future and they will assume their former activity, and again take their place in the production of wealth from the gold-bearing veins and the tilling of the soil. One might go on writing page after page, citing incidents of early

days, some merry, some sad, yet all cherished as
a memento of early days, but

> Farewell, to you
> Old mining camps of Time!
> Where once the desperado gambled
> And the forty-niner mined.
> Alas! No more these exciting scenes,
> As the placer gold has left the streams.
>
> Yes, yes; it all is true;
> For the old, old camps are replaced by new,
> The gray-haired pioneers, they, too, are through,
> And one by one they bid us adieu.
> So all farewell, farewell to you!

Thus I have briefly spoken of the early history
of California, and happily guided the reader over
the routes of the early explorers and venturesome
pioneers from the far east to the Golden Gate,
and to the gateway of El Dorado county, from
whose treasure vaults the gold was taken that
made California famous, and excited the world;
from whose rich soil will come forth superior
fruits; from whose dashing streams will be developed unlimited electric power; within whose
boundaries can be found the chief summer resorts
of the Sierras; and whose highway system and
roads will equal any in the mountain regions of
the State. She is possessed with a multiplicity of
features which must prove of advantage to her
rapid and permanent growth, and not the least
important is her climate.

Old El Dorado in 1851 had a population of
20,785, and in 1852, 40,000, about 4,000 more than
San Francisco had at that time. At a general
election in this year she polled 11,252 votes, being

the greatest number polled at that time in any county in the State. At the same election San Francisco polled 8,408 votes. She was represented in the Legislature from 1853 to 1856 by two Senators and eight Assemblymen. In 1860 the population had begun to decrease, being at this time only 20,582. This was due to the great rush to the Nevada Silver Bonanza strike which started about 1859 and continued until 1868. In 1870 she had a population of 10,309, increasing to 10,685 in 1880, and finally settling down to a steady population, with a slow but steady increase. It was during the early period that she acquired the proud title of "Empire County".

In May, 1858, the first overland stage coach operated by the Pioneer Stage Company between Placerville and Salt Lake City, made its appearance in old Hangtown, loaded down with human freight, and with mail from wife, mother, and fond ones at home, to the relative or friend in the mining camps of El Dorado, and in return would carry to the anxious ones in far away homes the glad tidings or sad news from those who had recently departed to the newly discovered gold fields in hopes of becoming rich and returning home. Each coach was driven by a daring driver who handled the reins that controlled the speed and course of six fiery horses, as they dashed over the summit and down the western slope of the Sierras, around the treacherous bends of the newly constructed grade, known as the "Johnson Cut-off", stopping at the different stations as follows: Phillips, Tavern,

Toll Gate, Sales, Bakers, Strawberry, What Cheer House, San Francisco House, Junction House, Dix, Websters, and on down across Brockliss bridge to Sportsman Hall, curving in and out along the banks of the picturesque American river canyon.

The drivers of these coaches were not always certain that each trip would be free from exciting

A PIONEER STAGE COACH.

scenes, a runaway, a spill-over-the-grade, or holdup by some highwayman, the latter being numerous along the roads and byways of the mining regions.

Many a young man, after repeated trials, failed to stake out a rich claim, lost all hopes, disheartened, turn traitor to his early teachings and took to robbing as a profession, holding up and taking from the successful, or relieving the new arrival

"HANK MONK."
Old Stage Driver.

of his past savings. One of the boldest and most
noted hold-ups on the overland route was that of

BULLION BEND,

June 30th, 1864, when the two coaches of the
Pioneer Stage Company, driven by Charley Watson and Ned Blair, were held up and robbed of
the mail and seven sacks of
bullion,—which was being
shipped from Virginia City,—
at a turn in the road about
two and one-half miles above
Sportsman Hall station. The
robbers failed to get the main
treasure-box of Wells, Fargo
& Company's express, it being on one of the other three
coaches that were yet to come.
Immediately on the arrival of
the two coaches at Placerville, Sheriff Rogers was in-
formed of the robbery, and
making up a posse composed
of Deputy Sheriff Staples, Constables Van Eaton,
and Ranney, and several others, started in pursuit
of the robbers. The posse was divided, Sheriff
Rogers and his men went direct to the scene of
the hold-up, while Staples, Eaton, and Ranney
took a road to the southeast in hopes of head-
ing off the robbers or picking up their tracks
on some of the cross roads leading from the
scene of the hold-up to the southern part of the

CHARLEY WATSON.
Pioneer Stage Driver.

"CURLEY DAN."   (B. B. BURCH.)
A Pioneer Stage Driver.

county. They succeeded in the latter and took the trail, following the bandits to Pleasant Valley, where Eaton was sent back to inform Sheriff Rogers of their discovery. Staples and Ranney continued on the trail, overtaking the robbers at the Summerset House, where a fight ensued, Staples being killed and Ranney dangerously wounded. The robbers were in a room in the house, and when Staples entered at the door, and demanded a surrender, his answer was the report of the bandits' revolvers. At the same instant Staples fired, and fell dead on the floor. His shot struck one of the robbers named Pool in the head, but did not kill him. After taking everything of value from the bodies of Staples, Ranney, and their wounded comrade, they fled, leaving the latter behind. About ten days later three out of the remaining five, who, on their way to their rendezvous in Santa

COON HOLLOW CHARLIE (CHARLES SADDLE)

Clara county, met a Sheriff and his posse on the lookout, who immediately attacked and a battle ensued, in which one of the trio was killed, another later died from his wounds, and the third was captured and brought back to Placerville, where he turned State's evidence and gave the names of his comrades, J. A. Robertson, Henry

Jarboe, George Cross, Wallace Glendenin, Joseph
Gamble, John Ingram, H. Gately, and Preston
Hodges. These men were later captured at their
rendezvous by Sheriff James B. Hume and Deputy
Van Eaton, brought back to Placerville, where
several were tried. Preston Hodges was found
guilty of murder in the second degree and sen-
tenced to twenty years in the State's prison, and
Poole, who was considered the better one of the
band, was found guilty of murder and was exe-
cuted September 29th, 1865. The balance got a
change of venue to Santa Clara county, where they
were tried and acquitted. Five sacks of bullion
were recovered, it having been hidden in various
ways and places near the scene of the robbery.

Another incident which is worthy of note and
connects itself with El Dorado county history and
the overland mail route was Horace Greeley's visit
to California. It was in the summer of 1867, and
the news of his coming had preceded him several
days, and being a distinguished gentleman, he was
received accordingly at each station. At the moment of taking his seat inside the stage coach at
Carson City, Horace spoke to the driver, Hank
Monk, informing him that it was necessary that
he be at Placerville on time, as he, Greeley, had
agreed to deliver a short address to its citizens
before departing for Sacramento. His stage was
due to leave Placerville on the arrival of the coach
on which he was a passenger. Monk answered
with a quick "Yes 'er", and at the crack of his whip

*Notes from Upton's Pioneers.

the coach gave a sudden lurch ahead and they were
off. The further they traveled the faster they
went, and the rougher it seemed to Horace, for
he was now no longer able to hold his seat. His
appeals to go slow were frequent, but to each Monk
replied: "Keep your seat, Horace. I'll get you
there on time", and he did, and just before the appointed time for their arrival at Placerville, they
were met by a committee of citizens on horseback,

OLD STRAWBERRY HOUSE.
Pioneer Stage Station and Resort, on Road Between Placerville,
Lake Tahoe and Carson City. Lovers' Leap Rock in the Distance.

and escorted into the city, where Mr. Greeley delivered a short address from the first veranda
of the old Cary House, and in the course of his talk
he told of this wonderful ride and repeated Monk's
words. Horace Greeley and Hank Monk have since
passed away, and the old historic hostelry which

has been the scene of many exciting times is now being razed* to make room for a more stately and up-to-date hotel. The old building was erected by William M. Cary, being completed in August, 1857.

A telegraph line was constructed across the Sierras from Hangtown to Carson in 1858 by the Placerville and Humboldt Telegraph Company, and the first and only railroad to date to enter the county was the continuation of the first railroad built in the State, the Sacramento Valley line, being first built to Folsom in 1855, then to Latrobe and finished to the old mining camp of Shingle Springs in 1866, the terminus of the road until May 25th, 1888, when it was completed into Placerville. The town of Latrobe was laid out by the field engineer of this road and named by him after the location engineer of the first railroad built in the United States. After the completion of the Central Pacific railway to California, 1868, the overland mail by stage was discontinued. At the same time the county practically became depopulated, owing to the easy method of returning home, for those who cared to go, and the rush to the other rich discoveries which were being frequently reported from other parts of the State, and the population that the Empire County once had has never returned. What has been said is only a glimpse of the past when old El Dorado ranked first in wealth and population among the counties of the State, but the placers of El Dorado could not last forever, yet this is what they have accomplished, the tide

*March 15th, 1915.

of emigration in the early fifties, surged toward
these treasure vaults. The great wave reached its
culmination and then burst into thousands of
fragments, scattering the spray all over the west.
Go north, go east, go south, and you will find the
results of El Dorado gold. Visit the great cities
of the west and ask who laid their foundations.
El Dorado county has furnished material that has
been and will ever be a great power in the building
up of the various industries of this western land.

To strong arms and brave,brave hearts she gave
her golden treasure, and bade them go forth and use
it in the building up of a mighty nation, and all she
asked in return was

REMEMBER THE GIVER.

But the past alone is not all that remains of
El Dorado. She has a present existence which
claims more than a passing attention. Although
the population of 1852 is not to be found among
her hills and valleys; although many of the miners'
cabins have fallen to decay, and only here and
there a heap of stones remains of the stone chim-
neys that stood at their backs; although a series
of tailing piles point out the exhausted surface
diggings, yet in the place of these you find other
evidences of activity and wealth in the El Dorado
of today, which shows a permanency not to be
found in those early times, when the pioneers
came here to get rich and return to their far-away
homes.

A golden past, an earnest present, and a promise for the future, whose magnitude we now cannot

divine, but which we trust will be in accord with
the vast possibilities of this glorious State. Meas-
ured from this standpoint old El Dorado stands the
test. Her territory we will now view with the
eye, not of the man of business, not with a pierc-
ing glance of the calculating, enterprising wealth
accumulated, but let us roam from valley to valley,
penetrate her secluded nooks and dells, ascend her
mountain peaks, and view what Nature has given
her. No place has Nature been more indulgent,
neither can you find a greater variety of scenery,
nor prospects more pleasing to the eye than within
the boundaries of this old county. And more, dotted
here and there in lonely gulch and on hill can be
found an occasional miner's cabin inhabited by
an old pioneer who, as an intrepid youth, crossed
mountain, plain and sea, to share the hidden wealth
of the new El Dorado; and whom various writers
have pictured as being a rough, uneducated person
of the wild west. But how untrue of the real
pioneer gold hunters who were the cream of American and European manhood. It is true these old
stragglers impress you strangely at first, and their
unwillingness to freely converse with you naturally
leads one to believe that they are uneducated. But
when you once come to know them you find that
many are graduates of a university, that their youth
was spent in a Christian home, and that their appearance and unwillingness to converse with you
is due to their having lived many years alone, their
cat and dog being their only companions. So they

continue to live and cling to the old sport, still hopeful and expectant.

What more can be said of the El Dorado of yesterday? Only this, "To the pioneer belongs the El Dorado of yesterday". His energy was expended here while in life's prime, and in many a quiet valley, on many a grassy slope he sleeps, after the bustle and excitement of the days of gold.

> Ah! when shall they all meet again?
> As in the days long since gone by.
> Can we give them too much homage?
> Have these great men any peers?
> No! ten million tongues declare it;
> God bless our brave old pioneers.

One by one we miss the familiar faces of these old heroes, as each one passes beyond our mortal vision. Let each one leave behind him a memory that we cherish as an inspiration which is to lighten our pathway through the coming years. The memory of his deeds urges us to greater endeavors, and thus he leaves a lasting heritage for all times.

Oh, pioneers! Glorious has been the dawning, and the beauties of the sunset will be no less magnificent.

> "Lo, when the last pick in the mine
> Lies idle, useless, rusting red,
> Sweet bards along this sunset shore
> Will tell in song of those who bled,
> And fearless faced the vast unknown
> O'er rocky peaks and desert sand,
> Or dauntless tread on unblazed trail
> That beckon'd to this golden land.

"In mellow lullabies they'll sing
Their sweetest songs as they entwine
The deeds wrought by these old men,
These mighty men of forty-nine.
They'll tell in song like ocean roar
Or cadence like its murmuring sand,
Of long agone there was a day
When there were giants in the land."

And the greatest of them all was James Wilson Marshall, who lived to see the world enriched by his discovery, while he himself wandered thereafter poor and homeless, so to say, over a land that neglected to repay her immense debt of gratitude to him who gave her all her wealth, power and position. As with all great benefactors of mankind, his name is recorded on historic page, while his body rests beneath a stately monument, not far distant from the old mill where he discovered the golden key that unlocked the resources of our State and laid the foundation of the El Dorado of today.

PART II.

CHAPTER I.

The El Dorado of Today and Her Resources.

A much favored land, famous in history as the seat of the first discovery of gold in the far west which was, before the discovery, a "raging wilderness", where nothing save the moaning winds and the noises emanating from the throats of the Digger Indians and wild animals broke the stillness and awakened the echoes. The news relating to the discovery of gold spread like wildfire throughout the whole world, and the contagion which is bred of money-seeking was so greatly felt, that during a few short months in the year 1849, the surface of the country was black with people from all climes, and probably not one of the thousands that visited this section of the west in the early days realized that it would some day be famous for its variety of rich and fertile soil, beautiful scenery, invigorating climate, vast forests of timber, mines, and natural wonders. Yet it is true, and throughout the western portion there are vast grazing lands and the Sierras in summer are green with native grasses affording the finest of pasture ranges. Fruit growing is conducted successfully, and almost every variety grows well.

Truthfully speaking, it is where the great pine shoots up its majestic trunk, crowned with evergreen leaves and scented with the fragrance of the forest; where the forest and hillsides are

adorned with blossoms of every hue; where the
golden poppy ornaments the gardens and orchards;
where a genial warmth seldom forsakes the atmosphere; where berries and fruits of all descrip-
tions are met with at every step; in a word, it is
where Nature seems to have paused as she passed
over the earth, and opening her stores, filled the
underlying rocks and soil with precious metals,
and to have strewn over the surface with unspar-
ing hand all the beauties she possessed. But where
did you say we could find this favored land? It is
in that great State of California to whose distant
shores the far east sent forth her adventurous sons,
to wrest for themselves a habitation from the wild
inhabitants of the forest, enrich themselves with
that golden metal and to convert the neglected
soil into fields of exuberant fertility. It is in that
historic old county of El Dorado that these boun-
ties of Nature are in the greatest perfection,
and it will not be many years before neat and
comfortable homes with every indication of
wealth and happiness about them, will be scattered throughout the valleys and as high up on
the mountain side as convenience of ingress will
permit. Summer homes will fill every nook in
the foothills and mountains, where the silence will
be broken by the merry laugh of the tourist, the
whoop of the mountain climber, and the honk,
honk of the automobile.

The surface of the county is a succession of
hills and dales, or, to speak with greater difference
to the geographical definition, of mountains and
valleys. It is in these mountains that the hun-

dreds of small streams take their rise; and, flowing from the limpid lakes and thousand springs,
the numerous sources of the American and Cosumnes meander through the hills to the valleys
below, where uniting their streams, they help form
the two great rivers of the State, the Sacramento
and San Joaquin.

The mountains are heavily timbered and accessible for most their height. Although instances
are not wanting where the sides are jutted with
rocks, that aid greatly in giving to the county that
romantic and picturesque character which it so
eminently possesses.

The valleys throughout the foothill country are
narrow and rich, with a water course uniformly
winding through each, and beautiful picturesque
homesites are found interspersed along the mar-
gins of the small lakes, or situated at those points
along the streams which are more favorable for
small farms. The scenery along the mountain
roads and streams has its charm and unsurpassing
beauty.

The mineral belt of this old county has produced millions of dollars. From the discovery of
gold to the end of the hydraulic period about 1885,
El Dorado carried the penant. The great "Mother
Lode" belt passes almost due north through the
county, and the eyes of the mining world are again
being turned to this undeveloped section, in so far
as deep gravel or quartz mining is concerned. And
when the key is discovered that will unlock this
great treasure vault which supplied the ravines,
rivers and gulches and scattered over the surface

of the sidehills the millions in gold that brought
fame to this venerabe old county, she will again
supply her portion of the world's wealth.

The most valuable minerals found in the county
are gold, silver, copper, iron and asbestus. Besides the enormous wealth in mineral ores, there
is a great variety of all kinds of valuable stones;
the granite of the Sierras; the limestone lodes that
cross from south to north through the western part
of the county; marble beds of a most excellent
quality abound a few miles south of Placerville,
and also near Indian Diggings in the southern part
of the county. Slate quarries are numerous in the
vicinity of Kelsey, and soapstone and asbestus
ledges are found here and there along the "Mother
Lode", a resource embracing wealth that may
rival at a not very distant day the former. Electro
silicon, another valuable mineral, has been found
in great quantities near Smith Flat. It is used
in cleaning silverware and metals of every description, and for this purpose it has no superior.
Cinnabar has been found near the southern boundary of the county, and salt in the Lake Valley
region.

Mining, no doubt, will continue to be one of
the great resources of this county, but each suc-
ceeding year more distinctly marks the boundary
between the two great pursuits, mining and agriculture. The former, steadily on the decline, leaves
but a wreck behind, without a shadow of hope for
recuperative energy. The latter steadily augments
the wealth of the county, affords constant employment, and permanent homes, cultivating not only

the rich valley land, but daily extending its lines toward the Sierras, up the ravines, gulches, and foothills, obliterating the old land marks of the surface miner, fencing, plowing, planting, and reaping over and around the deserted ditches, sluice-ways, tunnels, and shafts. So, too, year after year, the agricultural area of this county widens, and the fallacious notion of the early settler respecting the sterile nature of large portions of the county disappear. The truth is, that there is but a small portion of the area of El Dorado county that is not susceptible of cultivation or suited to grazing.

On the decline of placer mining in El Dorado county, after the pursuit of gold became less a fortuitous scramble for surface nuggets, and mining had come to demand skill, patience, and business methods, the hundreds that were left and who followed were turned to other pursuits, and from that period dates the permanent prosperity of the county, and development of the vast and varied resources of the soil, and since that time there has been an entirely different character of population—homeseekers with families instead of male fortune hunters who had no thought of permanent residence, but only to get rich quick and return to their homes in the far east. The former is the character of population that El Dorado county is looking for. They come not to tame a wilderness, but to enjoy such a land as travelers seek, where exists not only the most hospitable of climates, but the most generous land for homebuilding. It is they who will clear and till the

soil and plant groves of tropical fruits; instead
of building frontier cabins, they will erect a class
of homes such as probably cannot be found in any
other county with an equal population.

You may be sure the climate of old El Dorado
county is glorious. Her soil is of inexhaustible
fertility, her mountains still teem with untold
wealth, and the evergreen forest, beautiful lakes,
and crystal streams alive with trout, are factors
that must contribute largely to her continued
growth and prosperity. Thus speaks the voice of
Nature in

THE HIGH SIERRAS.

The grand old range that marks the eastern
boundary of California from north to south is
not, in El Dorado county, of the barren and desolate character that many might suppose. Thousands of acres are of the deep, rich soil, fit for
agriculture, with numerous small meadows from
which are cut large quantities of natural hay.
Here can be found the finest pasture ranges in
summer, that serve as a most welcome retreat
to the famished cattle and sheep which in great
numbers are driven up from the parched plains
during the summer months, and down its rugged
sides are the great forests.

The snowfall in this range begins toward the
end of November, and continues through the winter months until April, during which, upon the
high peaks and ridges, there is a snowfall of from
ten to twenty feet, becoming less and less as you

descend, disappearing altogether at an elevation of 3000 feet, except during an exceedingly cold storm, when the ground will become covered as far down as the 1500 foot elevation, but seldom, if ever, seen below this. The winter is over by April, when spring opens balmy and pleasant. By the middle of July not a trace of winter can be seen except in a few isloated spots throughout the higher peaks, where may be seen small patches of snow, as if dodging and hiding from the powerful rays of the sun, which through the long summer days pours down its scorching floods of light and heat.

Farming, lumbering, and grazing are carried on with success in El Dorado's portion of the Sierras, and it is yearly becoming the resort of the tourist. The air is pure, mild and refreshing. As summer passes and the valleys below are parched, these mountains still retain their verdure, and through the long, hot summer they are green, and their lakes and natural wonders, the resorts of thousands of pleasure seekers and inhabitants of the dusty plains, who stroll beneath the luxuriant foliage, angle in the streams, boat upon the placid waters, and gaze upon or climb the majestic columns of granite that form the mountain peaks, which lift their imposing heads above the clouds.

The important peaks of this range in El Dorado county are: Tells, Pyramid, Angora, Castle, Tallac, Dicks, Jacks, Rubicon, Silver, Friels, Phipps, Maggies, Ellis, and Twin, whose towering pinnacles and snow-capped crowns reflect their lengthened shadows upon the placid bosom of the queen of the Sierras,

LAKE TAHOE,

. The home of the tourist and El Dorado county's playground. The colors and transparency of this beautiful sheet of water attract the attention of the visitor. The green forests, the rugged cliffs that rise out of the water from great depths, and the hard, grayish sand that forms the shores on

LAKE TAHOE, EL DORADO COUNTY.

either side of this aerial urn, have been the theme of romantic poets, enthusiastic tourists, and sighing lovers. The water, which is a pea green, gradually deepens, leaving the bottom of the lake at from fifty to eighty feet clearly visible; a short distance from the shore the color changes with

the undulations of the bottom, first from a tinge
of blue to a deep green, then to a very deep green
and finally to an almost indigo blue. To appreciate the scenic features of this great mountain
lake which has a circumference of approximately
sixty miles, requires a trip upon its beautiful water
in one of the finely equipped passenger steamers,
which touch at the various resorts, or drive along
the State Highway which will soon girdle her
picturesque shores, or with saddle horse and guide,
ramble over the rough trails up the mountain sides
to the noted peaks. The coming years will behold
this rare gem of nature and its gorgeous scenery
as the recreation ground and watering place of
happy throngs of health and pleasure seekers.

Nature seems to have been more generous in
El Dorado's portion of this great mountain range,
for besides the many beautiful lakes and crystal
streams, there are a number of mineral springs
whose waters are noted for their medicinal qualities. Those that are accessible by good mountain
roads and near Lake Tahoe are the Soda Springs
on the Rubicon river and at the summit overlooking Fallen Leaf lake. The Sulphur and Soda
Springs on the western summit near Loon lake,
on the road that crosses the summit from Lake
Tahoe by the way of the Rubicon, following closely the route of the old Georgetown and Lake Bigler
(Tahoe) trail, and on down the western slope,
winding its way through the giant trees of the
forest, across streams and along the crest of ridges
that affords a grand view of the Rubicon River canyon, to Georgetown, Placerville and Sacramento,

and other points on the main line of railroad. Here
and there along this route are found an occasional
hotel and camping ground resorts, where each
summer are camped many families, and hunting
and fishing parties from the foothills and hot, sul-
try valleys.

The year 1915 will bring these beauties of
Nature and natural wonders of the Sierras nearer
to the tourist, for the State Highway and road
will cross this old historic county from west
to east, entering the South Fork of the American
River canyon a short distance above Placerville
and paralleling it to the summit of the range.
Along this ravishingly picturesque canyon are
numerous summer resorts where the traveler may
rest for a while and enjoy the pure mountain air.
Arriving at the summit the road descends to Lake
Valley, touching at the southern end of Lake Tahoe,
then on across the State line into Nevada. Being
for nearly its whole length the route of the
"pioneer" and the main route of the Lincoln Highway from New York to San Francisco. And again,
as of old, after crossing the dusty plains the traveler will be refreshed by El Dorado's

CLIMATE.

Being entirely in the foothills of the Sierra
Nevada mountains, El Dorado county's climate is
governed by this range. The western portion of
the county is by no means free from the heated
days of the summer months, and unless well irri-
gated, will become parched and dry. With all this,

the air becomes cool on the setting of the sun,
and the night which is almost cold, brings with it
its copious dews, which invigorate vegetation and
make the nights pleasant for sleeping, thereby
counteracting the great heat of the day, which
seldom reaches 90 degrees in mid-summer. However hot the air, it is not oppressive, and men
working in the open mines, and in the fields under
a scorching sun do not experience fatigue; it is
the cold nights, bracing atmosphere, genial climate, pure water, and the luxuriant fruits and
vegetables that surround the many happy homes
that are at present nestled in among the foothills
and mountains, whose prosperity attests the value
of old El Dorado county as a future place of permanent abode. The summers are dry and hot
from June to September, the spring and fall always pleasant. The winters are not very cold,
except in the higher mountains. The thermome-
ter never registers lower than 15 degrees above
zero in the western and central portion, with an
average winter temperature of 50 degrees, the real
winter months being December to April. The rainfall is light in the extreme western portion of the
county, and an average of sixty inches in the central portion with heavy snows in the eastern or
mountainous portion. About the middle of November, the rains begin to fall and the Sierras
receive their first fleecy robes of winter, the skirts
of which grow thin and ragged as they reach down
the western slope towards the valleys, until they
entirely disappear. While the tall pines of the
forest in the high elevations groan under their

burden of snow, and the cold, wintery winds sweep
over the jagged peaks, and the miner and woods-
man seek the shelter of their log cabins, and the
trapper and winter tourist make their tedious
journey up the mountain sides, or sweep down the
crusted glade on their narrow skis, the farmer
guides the plow in the foothills and in the valleys below; tender shoots of buds and grass welcome the refreshing showers, and waving grain
fields, blooming orchards and golden poppies pro-
claim the presence of spring, and the ravines and
streams of the foothills afford an abundance of
water for irrigation and

MINING.

Mountain regions have long been the seat of
important mining industries, and it was from the
treasure vaults of the western slope of the Sierras
in El Dorado county, that set the world to think-
ing in 1848, when gold was discovered and the
rich placers and river beds were vigorously worked,
and gold could be found on the sides and ravines of
the foothills, the summits of the ridges, in the soils
of the gardens and fields, the bed and sand bars
of living and ancient rivers, every available spot
of this class swarmed with thousands of gold
seekers, who, with prospecting pan, shovel and
rocker, sluicing the flats, gulches and hillsides,
have discovered and pretty thoroughly worked most
of the accessible surface diggings of the county.
Then came the discovery and working of the gravel
beds of ancient rivers, and the working of the great

seam diggings by the hydraulic and tunnel methods. But this method of mining met the disapproval of the valley farmers, who vigorously protested, and in 1882 the Legislature passed a bill prohibiting this method of mining. The act was the means of locking up, in the hills of the Sierras of El Dorado county, untold wealth that could only be profitably mined by the hydraulic method. Hydraulicing was and is still carried on in some sections not covered by the law, and in those sections where impounding dams are placed in the streams, below the working pits, to hold back the debris. In this method of mining the water is delivered under high pressure from a movable and pivoted nozzle, sometimes called a "monitor" or "giant", against the bank of auriferous material, and the detached debris washed into sluice-ways where the gold is separated and deposited. These sluices are long and narrow flumes, being sometimes three to five feet in width, and eighteen inches to two feet in depth, the bottoms of which are always paved with round blocks, from three to six inches thick, with a diameter equal to the width of the flume, or narrow strips of wood or iron laid transversely or longitudinally on the bottom, called "riffle bars", between which are recesses for collecting the gold.

Some of these flumes are upwards of a mile long. Mercury is often fed in at the upper end to assist by its coating properties in collecting the gold. Clean-ups are made every few days, when the water is turned off, the riffles removed and the gold and amalgam recovered, retorted, and molded into gold bars, afterwards sent to the mint and coined into money. Although this method of mining is considered the cheapest, it requires an immense water supply, which is often brought for miles in ditches or flumes at a great expense. I have before spoken of the exhausted placers. This is true when speaking of the open or stream placers, but not so when applied to the hidden treasures of the seam belts. Placer mining is but one form of searching for gold, and is the class of mining most easily worked, and with the least expenditure of capital. Along the seam belts of the "Mother Lode", mines of great richness are constantly being developed. In many cases, pockets of pure gold have been and are yet being found, having a value of from $500 to $25,000. Along the "Mother Lode" belt from Placerville to Kelsey, Garden Valley and Georgetown, are found many of these rich quartz seams, which form a network between the walls of this great mineral belt. The mines at Georgia Slide, one and a half miles north of Georgetown, are in this belt, and have been worked for more than fifty years, and are still working and paying.

Quartz and lode mining closely followed the discovery of gold, and quartz ledges of all sizes and richness have been discovered in many parts of the county, but especially along the "Mother Lode" belt, which parallels the summit of the Sierras and crosses the county from south to north. Once the merry music of the quartz mills broke the silence of the canyon and hillside as their ponderous stamps fell, one after another, on the rich ore taken from the ledges most easily worked.

PLACER MINING IN THE FAMOUS GEORGIA SLIDE SEAM MINES.

Today there are but few, and many partially developed ledges exist, waiting for the capital which is needed to release the captive metal from its rocky prison below the surface, and send it abroad to do its work in the world. El Dorado county is still a land of gold, and the amount taken from her mines at the present time is by no means insignificant. Nor is gold the only mineral found within her boundaries.

Copper ore has been discovered in many localities, beds of crome iron are also abundant. And asbestus of a fine texture has been found in the northern part of the county. They exist in quantities that would compensate one for the labor spent in obtaining them. Some day in the near future, when this great treasure vault is to be unlocked, and its copper, its iron, its granite, its marble, its gold, and other valuable minerals which it contains are needed in the fulfillment of the Creator's design, man will be given the colossal key to unlock and swing open the gates, and permit these valuable treasures to be taken from the recesses where they have rested for ages, waiting the appointed time.

All of this can be done much more economically in this county than in most of the mining regions, owing to the unlimited water supply which can be used for power, either directly through its pressure applied to impulse or turbine wheels, or indirectly through its conversion into electric energy brought from distant points along the streams. It has so cheapened mining that many low grade deposits heretofore worked at a loss can now be profitably

AMONG THE GIANT THEES OF EL DORADO'S FOREST.
(By Courtesy of "American Lumberman.")

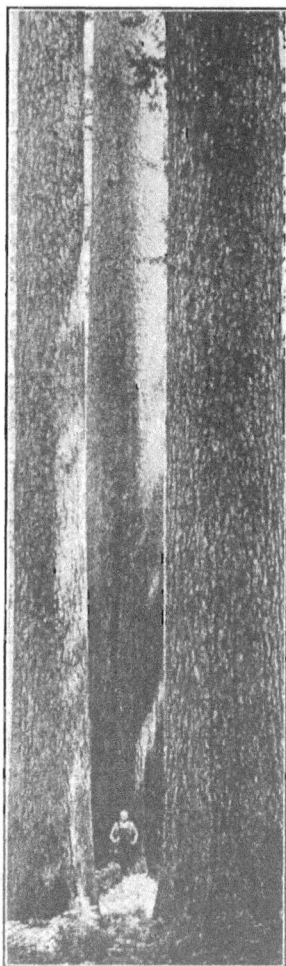

SUGAR PINE.

mined. Timbers and lagging used for underground timbering and supports can be had at a reasonable figure owing to the nearness of the

FOREST.

Continuing upward from the great valley at the base of the Sierras, one enters the mountains proper; and at an elevation of 2500 feet beholds the vast forest of El Dorado county, the extent of which can only be realized by fixing the mind upon the whole area covered with this somber green, that extends north and south across the county, where the traveler may roam among the giant trees of many species, standing close together, so as to almost shut out the sunlight. As one continues the ascent, and passes the 6000 foot elevation, they leave the conifers behind, crowded out by the rocky slopes and cold, wintery climate. Instead they find the tamarac here and there around the meadows and small lakes, and the great red fir upon the drier slopes. There is evidence that the forest at one time covered the surface of the county from the dry timber line where there was not sufficient moisture to support tree life, to the wet timber line, which is very pronounced at about the 6000 foot elevation. The lower or present timber line is at about the 2500 foot contour. Between these two timber lines stand large quantities of the finest timber, in which can be found the sugar and yellow pines, the cedar and fir, the oak and spruce, in such numbers and variety, and beauty as to bewilder the mind. The sugar and California

CALIFORNIA WHITE PINE

white, or so-called yellow pine, are the growth of
centuries, and help greatly towards the 5,000,000,-
000 feet of lumber that these forests contain. As
civilization advanced towards the higher mountains, small sawmills were erected to supply the
local demand, and now the echo of the wood-

THE OLD WAY.
In the Forest of El Dorado.

man's ax, the roar of the stately trees as they
strike the ground, and the screeching of the log-
ging trains as they wind in and out of the canyons on their way to the mills, are familiar sounds

to the many that visit these great forests. All of this for money? Most true. The large lumber companies are fast eating their way into the more and more remote districts, and ere long the great sugar pine belt, the pride of El Dorado's inhabitants, will be tapped and the noble trees which have been hundreds of years in attaining their present size will soon disappear. To say soon, is not meant in a few months, nor in a few years, but within the next century, for the lumberman of today is not to be compared with the pioneer lumber butcher, who recklessly skinned, then abandoned their cut over sections, with no thought of the future or the effect upon the water resources. It is no longer a question of doubt that plant life protects and helps to preserve the underground waters, The lumber companies of today are more careful, and prize their timber holdings more highly, and in many places assist the general government in their work of preserving the young forest trees, which will in many cases, mature to commercial size within one hundred to one hundred and twenty-five years. These grand old monarchs of the land would seem to have perished with grief on beholding the ravages of man. But there is an aristocracy existing in these woods at the present day, for it has been observed that there are different classes of trees—families of nobility clustering together in one place—while the more plebeian varieties congregate in communities by themselves. Were it not for the changing seasons and its living creatures, the monotony of this forest scenery would be well-nigh unbearable; but

summer fills every sunny nook with its bright
flowers, and winter scatters everywhere the fan-
tastic creations of the frost and snow. It was in
these solitudes that the bold and hardy Digger
Indian hunter tracked the native deer, and set his
traps for the wildcat and mink, the marten and
other small animals; and listened to the songs of
the native birds whose whole life, it seems, is
devoted to singing, in a kind of monotone, about
the joys of the wilderness.

Behold with what exquisite taste and skill Nature interposes her relief! She scatters throughout the great forest thousands of crystal streams
of the clearest and purest water; bids a few mountain peaks rise up as watch towers against the
eastern sky. But more than this: around the
lakes and along the water courses are permitted
to grow as great a variety of the more delicate
and graceful trees as the climate will allow, with
shrubs and vines and flowers innumerable. All
this is the workmanship of Nature; but it is man
who marks the earth with ruin, and, not content
with robbing the forest of their giant treasures,
he sometimes sets them on fire for his amusement,
or by accident, and thus comes into existence the
desolate burnt districts to take the place of trees
once valuable, and grand, and beautiful.

It is important, then, that the people in general
should assist the government in trying to retain
the forest, while at the same time taking from their
midst the matured timber for the necessary lumber
needed for the various industries, and to also be

of a remunerative benefit to the district to which the forest belongs.

The verdure of the forest is everlasting, and its beauty cannot be expressed in words. Therefore, we must learn to appreciate the beauties and wonders of the earth upon which we live, to foster the love of nature, and the out-of-door life, and it is of the utmost importance that the rugged mountain parts of the county and those noted for their attractive scenic features, together with their animal and plant inhabitants, be preserved in their natural state, so far as public necessity will permit. El Dorado county's rugged Sierras with their scenic features; her mines with their golden wealth, and her forest with all its verdure and beauty, must fall before the kings of all resources,

AGRICULTURE AND HORTICULTURE.

Throughout the central portion of El Dorado county there are enumerable beautiful and fertile valleys; and the foothills and rolling, gravelly ridges, heretofore supposed to be worthless, are the finest fruit lands that can be found anywhere in the west. Year after year the arable lands of the county seem to widen, mountain ridges and high rolling hills, regarded as worthless a few years since, are found by experience to be excellent farm lands, producing grain, vegetables, and fruits of every description, and under a diversified cultivation, and the agricultural skill and labor of experienced farmers and fruit growers, thousands of

acres, yet considered worthless, will be made most
productive. Fruit growing has become one of the
great resources of El Dorado county, and throughout the central portion is successfully conducted.
Almost every variety grows well. The berries are
equal to any grown in the State, and in the vicinity of Georgetown, in the northern part of the
county, the cherries are grown with a size and
flavor unsurpassed by any in the world. The pear,
prune, olive, peach, walnut, and apple grow well
on this divide, which includes the Greenwood,
Cool, and Pilot Hill districts. The warmth of this
plateau, which extends from the Sacramento valley to the Sierras, and the richness of its soil, well
adapt it to fruit culture. Those sections in the
vicinity of Placerville, Camino, Gold Hill, Coloma,
Lotus, and El Dorado, are noted for their excellent
fruits and berries of all kinds. Fruit growing as
a business has gained a foothold on the Placerville
divide, and hundreds of acres of her fertile soil
are being planted to golden fruits, and ere long
orchards and vineyards will cover the slopes as
far as the eye can see. The Fruit Growers' Asso-
ciation has been organized, and the fruits are being standardized, and carload after carload of the
finest fruit in the world is sent across the continent to the great cities on the shores of the At-
lantic. El Dorado county is also one of the grape
producing counties of California, and vineyards of
luscious grapes are plentiful along the foothill
sections of the western part of the county.

The soil of the agricultural districts is composed
of the broken and disintegrated slates, and allied

rocks mixed with varying portions of decayed and decaying animal and vegetable matter which makes a ferruginous soil of fine texture, and in many places on the higher plateaus and ridges there is a deep covering of volcanic ash, which is well adapted to the growing of various fruits, especially pears and apples. In speaking of the fruit possibilities of El Dorado county, many questions have been asked: Why has not the county advanced in fruit growing? Why have not the old farmers and fruit growers of the county become independent? To these questions the answer is, "that fruit growing as a distinct phase of agriculture is of comparatively recent development in America, and the efforts of the early settlers with orchard fruits, were devoted chiefly to the introduction of such as would yield a supply for the family of the owner, rather than to develop a commercial industry. To be successful in fruit growing, one must be skilled in fruit culture. Without proper cultivation and care, the fruits will degenerate back to their natural state, reproducing themselves only. There is no doubt that if the arts of cultivation were abandoned for only a few years, all the annual varieties of plants in our gardens would disappear and be replaced by a few wild forms. A close observation of the old house orchards in this county is answer enough to an experienced fruit grower as to El Dorado county's past history in fruit growing and farming, hence the necessity for constant and vigilant cultivation. This knowledge has been grafted into the old fruit growers of the county by the recent publications on fruit growing and the arrival of new people, experienced in fruit culture, and it has already had its effect in the fruit districts, and those who are following the new methods are becoming more independent each year. The list of fruits that can be grown in the county comprises all the varieties of peaches and nectarines, plums, prunes, apricots, apples, and pears, figs, and olives, walnuts, almonds and chestnuts, all the varieties of wine and table grapes do well, and in a few exceedingly warm, sheltered nooks on the western side of the county, some varieties of the orange are grown. This county also has the distinction of being the only county in the State where tea has been successfully raised. About the summer of 1869, a German, skilled in tea growing in Japan, founded a colony of Japanese tea farmers near Gold Hill, about five miles from Placerville, on the old Coloma road. Here the soil was sandy and rather dry, and the tea plants set out, grew well, and from samples raised, it was certain that tea could be successfully grown. The soil and climate of this vicinity for the growth and curing of tea were at this time pronounced unequalled in the world, but the enterprising German had to abandon his plantation at this period, owing to financial trouble, invasion of the miner, and the limited market for his product. This ended the first attempt at tea growing in this county. Were it possible at this time to present accurate statistics regarding the amount of fruit raised in El Dorado county, it would be a very favorable showing, for every variety flourishes here and attains the fullest degree of perfection. Even

at an altitude of 4000 feet you will find some of
the finest apples ever grown.

Irrigation is a necessity for the production of
fruits, of which the El Dorado of today can con-
sistently boast in terms of enthusiasm and pride,
for in all markets where the products of her soil
have been introduced, they have acquired a reputation both for quality and size, that is truly en-
couraging. El Dorado county's agricultural success is due to her climate and her numerous ever-
flowing

STREAMS.

As the old Sierras are accountable for El Dorado
county's beautiful and healthful climate, her natural wonders, mineral wealth, rich and fertile soil,
vast forests and grazing lands, so has she given
to her an unlimited supply of pure, clear, cold
water for domestic, agricultural, and power purposes, which is distributed over the surface of the
county by numerous dashing streams, fed by
springs from Nature's underground reservoirs and
the melting snows of the Sierras, and after uniting
their waters, help form the three main rivers of
the county, the two branches of the American and
the Cosumnes. Owing to the course and elevation
of these streams, the water can be taken out by
artificial canals, and distributed over nearly every
foot of tillable land in the county. There are at
present three water companies operating in the
county, one on the Georgetown divide, taking water
from Loon lake, and various streams along its
course. The main canals and feeders belonging

to this system cover the whole of the Georgetown
divide from the Sierras to the Pilot Hill district,
near the western boundary of the county. The
second and largest water system of the county is
that system which brings water from Echo and
Silver lakes and the South Fork of the American
river down the Placerville divide, supplying all the
farmers and miners along this ridge and the City
of Placerville with water. The third and most
southerly of the water systems operating in this
county is the one which takes its water from the
north branch of the Cosumnes river, supplying the
farms, orchards, and mines along its course, which
is along the south slope of the Placerville divide,
terminating near the town of Shingle Springs.
The consumers along these systems receive their
water for irrigation or mining use, either directly
from the main trunk canals or the laterals running
out from the main feeder to the place of use, and
it is sold to them by the "miners' inch". A "miners'
inch" is an expression which came into use during
the early mining days, and designates the amount
of water which will flow through an opening one
inch square, under a given pressure. The California statute inch is under a four-inch pressure, and
is equal to one-fiftieth of a cubic foot per second
flow, or the amount that will flow through the
opening in one second of time. The California
"miners' inch" is under a six-inch pressure, and is
equal to one-fortieth of a cubic foot per second
flow. The price per inch ranges from ten to thirty
cents per "miners' inch" per day service. A

day's service is divided into ten-hour service or
twenty-four-hour service.

The old proverb, "Water is life" is true, for
without it no human, animal or plant life can exist
for any length of time. Animals can move from
place to place in search of it, but plants must remain and adapt themselves to the surroundings
where they are planted, hence the importance of
irrigation. It has been carried on by man from
time immemorial, and has this advantage over the
natural rainfall, in that its application can be controlled and the growing crops can receive their
proportion of moisture just at the time they need
it most.

Water has made a paradise of portions of the
barren deserts of California, and without it, many
parts of the State would still be in its wild state.
There are portions of El Dorado county where the
moisture is sufficient to support plant life, but
there are other portions which require irrigation
in order to secure good crops. Certain parts of
the county which heretofore would only support a
few cattle have been made most productive, and
lands which have been used for the growing of
wheat, oats, and barley have been planted to fruit,
or alfalfa, making the owner thereof independent.
The truth is, that the interest which involves the
destiny of this promising county is dependent on
these beautiful and valuable streams. Without
their presence the many blooming orchards, fields
of alfalfa, the mills and the mines, and the hum

of the electric plants would be represented by desolation and waste.

These streams are also waiting the hands of skilled labor and capital to call them into turning the wheels of an active manufacture, which must at some day not far distant form an important branch of industry of the State of California; for furnishing cities and electric railways with electricity and for light and power purposes; nor are these magnificent water powers subject to the pinchy frosts of winter, which for so many months in the year, bind up the forces of the streams, clog the wheels, and hold in icy embrace the industry of large sections of the eastern and middle west states. Along these streams and around the small lakes that form their source are many flats and meadows of natural grasses which are valuable for

DAIRYING AND STOCK RAISING.

Dairy and stock raising are the last but not least of the many resources of El Dorado county. This industry has been developed only to a small part of its total possibilities. Yet, the county ranks high in her annual dairying and beef returns. Her reputation and wealth in dairying and stock raising are due to her exceptionally uniform climate, and the nutritious grasses of luxuriant growth on her vast area of grazing lands which lay along the western border of the county, in the vicinity of Shingle Springs, Latrobe, Clarksville, Nashville, and on the Summerset and Fairplay ridges. Hundreds of cattle and sheep are raised and pastured here in the winter, and ranged in the high Sierras during the summer months.

Poultry in great numbers are also raised in those sections of the county just named, and it is almost certain that these industries at a period not far distant will be increased many times their size.

SCHOOLS.

The wealth of the mining, agriculture, and stock raising sections of the county contribute to the up-keep of many little hamlets, most of which were settled during the early mining days, there being but one new town in the county, Camino, the terminal of the Placerville and Lake Tahoe rail-road, and situated six miles above Placerville on the State Road. But Placerville, Georgetown, and Mud Springs (El Dorado) remain the towns of commercial importance, and old Coloma, the his-toric center.

Within the last twenty years, the schools of El Dorado county have made extraordinary progress, and now rank ahead of most counties of her class. All instruction is now on the graded list, promo-tion and graduation examinations have been pro-vided, comprehensive and modern courses of study are in use and the teaching staff has been ma-terially strengthened.

Following the most advanced part of Califor-nia system, the schools are divided into two classes, elementary and secondary. Of the ele-mentary grade there are sixty schools, again sub-divided into summer and winter schools. The winter schools begin in September and run till

June; the summer schools begin in March and run
till November usually. This classification is necessary that instruction may be provided during the
months when weather conditions make it most
desirable to hold sessions. The El Dorado county
High School takes care of all secondary work,
serving all parts of the county efficiently.

The Board of Supervisors realizing that education should be provided for the few as well as for
the many, have been indulgent in forming and
maintaining school districts wherever the minimum
number of children reside; and as a consequence
modern school houses are within easy reach of
everybody. This Board has also been liberal when
providing funds, so that teachers' salaries and
school equipments are ample.

Aside from the regular course where pupils are
prepared for work in State Universities, the High
School furnishes a commercial course of instruction, where young people may prepare themselves
for business life. This feature of secondary school
work includes everything taught in the best business college and is very popular.

With a strong teaching staff, an efficient corps
of officers, with the most modern ideas well to the
front and ample money to carry out all plans with
merit in them, El Dorado county is justly proud
of her school system and invites comparison with
that of other sections of California concerning
which much more has been said and written.

PLACERVILLE.

The City of Placerville, a more appropriate and

prettier name, "Ravine City", is situated on the
banks of Hangtown creek, and is centrally located
in the county of El Dorado, of which it is the county
seat. It is the eastern terminus of the Sacramento
and Placerville branch of the Southern Pacific
railroad, fifty miles distant from Sacramento, the
capital of the State of California. The place was
the outgrowth of 'the mining excitement incident
to the discovery of rich placer diggings on old
Hangtown creek, and dates its existence from
1849. Four years following the first of the tide of
immigration, which poured ceaselessly for months
into this, then remote quarter, witnessed an in-
corporation of the place, at which time it had assumed all the importance of a dignified commercial
metropolis. It now has a population of two thousand whose intelligence and kindly natures are
reflected from frank and open countenances. The
new Court House, which has replaced the old
pioneer building, recently destroyed by fire, is a
large and comfortable building. This old town
in an early day was the scene of many exciting,
bustling incidents to the richness of the surface
mining in the vicinity, though at present nothing
in comparison can be seen. The elements so essential to the steady and substantial development of
a city are found in this locality in the form of good
fruit, grazing, and agricultural soil, plenty of good
water and timber and a pure, stimulating atmosphere. Its natural advantages for a permanent and
steady growth are of such a nature and so multi-
farious as to warrant the belief that the place will
become a city of considerable importance in a

period not very remote. The opportunities for developing the fruit growing, stock raising, and general agricultural interests are manifold. These facts are being taken advantage of yearly by persons who engage in the pursuits of the husbandman. New lands are being opened up, and an increase in the acreage planted to fruit and otherwise cultivated is annually being made. The old historic place will soon be connected with the capital of the State by a State Highway, being already connected with Lake Tahoe by the State Road. These two great arteries of travel will then be united by this city, the connecting link, and in 1915 made the route of the Lincoln Highway which will wind its way through a country made up of picturesque hills and dales, dotted with charming country homes, and along the route from Placerville to Lake Tahoe, the ever-changing and beautiful scenery makes the trip one of constant pleasure.

The town has ample drainage by Hangtown creek, which passes through its entire length.

The citizens of Placerville, or I will persist in calling it "Ravine City", are endowed with a spirit of energy and public improvement that adds greatly to their high recommendations of intelligence and morality. The public schools are spoken of in the highest terms, a perfect system for the education of pupils seeming to be the result most sought after. All religious denominations are represented, and an old, substantial banking firm supplies the residents with capital, never once forgetting the welfare of the citizens of their city and county. Two newspapers, the "Republican" and "Democrat", the former being a daily and weekly, and the latter a weekly, furnish the people with local and general news, both being ably conducted under efficient managers. Water is supplied by a splendid system of water works, and the streets and buildings are lighted with electricty, delivered to the city from the great power lines of a large power company a short distance away. The business houses as a rule are substantial and neat structures; with strictly up-to-date stocks. She has an array of hotels and restaurants; a good and efficient fire department; two lumber yards, planing mill, box factory, and foundry, which give employment to many mechanics. Two sanatoriums and an array of medical talent, and nearly all the fraternal organizations are represented here. It is also the terminus of three daily stage lines, one tri-weekly, and an efficient R. F. D. system. It is the home of the County Board of Trade, the members of which represent the fruit growing, agricultural and business interests of the county. The Board maintains a public reception room on the main business street that contains an exhibit of county products, which is a credit to the county and deserves attention by all who visit this city.

The Southern Pacific branch railroad was completed and the first train (an excursion train from San Francisco) was run into Placerville May 25th, 1888, on which occasion a fitting reception was

given under the auspices of the citizens of El Dorado county.

The fact that Placerville is the county seat of
the El Dorado of today is an assurance that it will
attract the bulk of the trade of the county. She
is the only city of any importance on the Lincoln
Highway after crossing the State line from Nevada
into California, and before arriving at Sacramento.
The mining interests, which have for some time
been at low ebb, are picking up with development
of quartz and gravel discoveries of late, and all
together the prospects are bidding fair to make her
one of the most important foothill towns of California.

GEORGETOWN.

The town of Georgetown, second in size in the
county, is situated upon the beautiful ground on the
dividing ridge between the South and Middle Forks
of the American river, about ten miles from the
former and five miles from the latter, and sixteen
miles north of Placerville. It is a picturesque
little village with a present population of about
five hundred, among whom are many families.
Pretty cottages, surrounded with pleasant flower
gardens, vines, fruit and shade trees, are to be
seen in every direction, giving it a pleasant and
prosperous appearance, convincing the most cas-
ual observer that its inhabitants have full confi-
dence in its permanence. The plateau upon which
it is situated is picturesque, commanding a grand
view of the Sacramento valley and the snow-clad
peaks of the Sierras. It is centrally located in

one of the most properous mining districts in the
State. The surrounding hills and gulches at one
time were the source of an abundant mineral supply. From the first settlement of this place, it
has been noted for its rich mines, many of the
gulches in the vicinity here yielded almost fabulous amounts to their fortunate workers. There
seems a greater degree of lasting permanence to
the mines about here than in most placer diggings,
and they seem likely to afford profitable employment for many years to the patient, enterprising
miner.

Agriculture in the vicinity of Georgetown has
attained an importance worthy of notice. As late
as 1856 the lands about here were regarded worthless. The gold mines and timber were supposed
to be all that were valuable. A few experiments,
conducted on a limited scale, however, led to the
belief that something might be done in regard to
agriculture. The small efforts at raising garden
vegetables were in many cases successful, and the
very few peach, apple, and cherry trees planted
by the miners seemed to grow rapidly and produce
excellent fruits, and the result has been that great
interest has been taken in the tilling of the soil
and the planting of orchards, and it is only necessary to ride about a circuit of a few miles in this
locality to be satisfied that those pursuits will soon
become, if not already, the predominating interest
in this neighborhood. The town is supplied with
water works that give to its inhabitants clear,
pure water, brought from the unpolluted streams
of the Sierras. The little village is well supplied

with up-to-date stores, one good hotel, a good
school, fraternal orders, and two churches, the
Catholic and Methodist, and one newspaper, the
"Gazette", which supplies the inhabitants with
local and county news. Among all the varied climates of California there are but few that can
claim precedence over Georgetown. Being on a
dividing ridge, it is seldom visited by untimely
frosts, the temperature rarely sinking below 30
degrees in winter or rising above 90 degrees in
summer. The town has daily stage communication
with Placerville, and with Auburn in Placer county.
A line of railroad which is greatly needed for the
transportation of lumber, that sooner or later the
timber belt of this divide will be called upon to
produce, and the large quantities of fruit that
are being yearly raised, is under advisement and
universally encouraged, and the lapse of a short
time, we doubt not, will witness the entrance of a
screeching locomotive, or the buzz of an electric
train into this town of bright promise. Summing
up the present situation and future prospects of
this place, we are led to believe that there are but
few towns that have more to encourage its inhabitants to hope for a healthy, rapid growth than
this beautiful mountain town which, as a resort
for pleasure and health, cannot be excelled.

EL DORADO.

This old, historic town is situated on the Sacramento and Placerville branch of the Southern

Pacific railroad, and also on the State Highway, fourteen miles from Placerville. Its main supports are the stock, mining and agricultural interests of the locality, which are very valuable. The town is somewhat "old timey" in appearance, but it is built on a healthy site with a beautiful surrounding country that presents a spectacle of luxuriance, comfort and ease. It possesses a good hotel, several stores, and is the terminal point of the stage line that runs into Amador county. It is also the commercial center of this district, and the people of the town and community look for a future greater than anything in the past.

COLOMA.

The last of the old historic towns to mention, but by no means the least important, is Coloma, a pretty place situated in the little valley from which it derived its name, not far distant from the river's edge, where once the ring of the pick, the chatter of thousands, and the scenes of exciting times never to be forgotten, but since that time, the old town has been steadily on the decline. Yet it is Coloma; and yet the site of the old mill and the raceway where gold was discovered can be pointed out. In a few years more, however, the oldest inhabitant will have passed away, all traces of the spot will be lost, and the visitor will be only able to discover that the gold was found "somewhere hereabout". The site of the old mill should be marked in an enduring manner, so as not to lose

forever a relic of a time which grows in interest
and in value as it recedes into the past.

Old Coloma should be cherished by all the world
as a memento of olden times, for it is the corner-
stone of this great commonwealth, wherein are in-
scribed many historical events. Could but Marshall
return and enlighten the world of the fruit possibilities and the rich agricultural surroundings of
which the Coloma valley can honorably boast, and

COLOMA IN 1857.
The X Indicates Where the Old Mill Stood.

start a migration of homeseekers to this golden
land, to till her soil and add to her population!
All the varieties of fruit grown in this valley and
on the surrounding hills are of superior quality.
As the El Dorado of today moves onward so may
old Coloma, until her inhabitants will witness a

repetition of her early past, not due to her gold, but to her golden fruit.

If a diversity of resources, such as El Dorado county is fast becoming noted for, can contribute to a rapid and permanent growth, then her near future will be crowned with that glory. Her destiny will place her in the front ranks of the prosperous counties of California.

What more can be said of the El Dorado of today? First came the gift of gold, millions after millions of dollars she has scattered abroad to do its work in the world. Then followed the natural production of her prolific soils which are ever increasing, and then her enchanting scenery which rivals that of the fairest clime, which will soon be viewed by thousands as they travel over the Lincoln Highway across the county from east to west. Thrice favored land. Let us cherish the memory of the past and welcome the dawning of a bright tomorrow.

THE END.